The Fear of God

THE FEAR OF GOD.

THE FEAR OF GOD.

THE

FEAR OF GOD.

BY JOHN BUNYAN.

FIRST PRINTED A. D. 1679.

LONDON:

THE RELIGIOUS TRACT SOCIETY;

Instituted 1799.

SOLD AT THE DEPOSITORY, 56, PATERNOSTER ROW,
AND 65, ST. PAUL'S CHURCHYARD;

AND BY THE BOOKSELLERS.

1839.

17.

[In preparing this volume for the press, a few obsolete words have been changed, and the references to Scripture have been carefully verified.]

CONTENTS.

THE FEAR OF GOD.

FEAR GOD. REV. XIV. 7.

CHAPTER I.

OBJECT AND REASONS OF FEAR.

THIS exhortation is not only found here in the text, but is in several other places of the Scripture pressed, and that with much vehemency, upon the children of men, as in Eccles. xii. 13; 1 Pet. ii. 17. I shall not trouble you with a long preamble, or fore-speech to the matter, nor shall I here meddle with the context, but shall immediately fall upon the words themselves, and briefly treat of the fear of God.

The text, you see, presents us with matter of the greatest moment, to wit, with God, and with the fear of him.

First, it presents us with God, the true and living God, Maker of the worlds, and Upholder of all things by the word of his power; that incompre-hensible Majesty, in comparison of whom all nations

B

are less than the drop of a bucket, and than the
small dust of the balance. This is he that fills
heaven and earth, and is every where present with
the children of men, beholding the evil and the
good; for he hath set his eyes upon all their ways.

So that considering that, by the text, we have
presented to our souls the Lord God and Maker of
us all, who also will be either our Saviour or Judge,
we are in reason and duty bound to give the more
earnest heed to the things that shall be spoken, and
be the more careful to receive them, and put them in
practice; for, as I said, as they present us with the
mighty God, so they exhort us to the highest duty
towards him; to wit, to fear him. I call it the
highest duty, because it is, as I may call it, not only
a duty in itself, but, as it were, the salt that seasons
every duty. For there is no duty performed by
us, that can by any means be accepted of God, if it
be not seasoned with godly fear. Wherefore the
apostle says, " Let us have grace, whereby we may
serve God acceptably with reverence and godly fear,"
Heb. xii. 23. Of this fear I would discourse at this
time; but because this word fear is variously taken
in the Scripture, and because it may be profitable to
us to see it in its variety, I shall choose this method
for the managing of my discourse, even to show you
the nature of the word in its several, especially of
the chief, acceptations.

I. Then by this word fear, we are to understand
God himself, who is the object of our fear.

II. By this word fear, we are to understand the
word of God, the rule and director of our fear.

I. Now, to speak of this word fear, as it is thus
taken, it respects God himself, who is the object
of our fear.

By this word fear, as I said, we are to understand God himself, who is the object of our fear; for the Divine Majesty goeth often under this very name himself. This name Jacob called him by, when he and Laban chode together on Mount Gilead, after Jacob had made his escape to his father's house: " Except," said he, " the God of my father, the God of Abraham, and the Fear of Isaac, had been with me, surely thou hadst sent me away now empty." So again, a little after, when Jacob and Laban agreed to make a covenant of peace with each other; though Laban, after the jumbling way of the heathen by his oath, puts the true God and the false together, yet " Jacob sware by the Fear of his father Isaac," Gen. xxxi. 42, 53. By the Fear, that is, by the God of his father Isaac.

And, indeed, God may well be called the Fear of his people, not only because they have by his grace made him the object of their fear, but because of the dread and terrible majesty that is in him. He is " a great and terrible God," and " with God is terrible majesty," Neh. i. 5; iv. 14; ix. 32; Job xxxvii. 22.

Who knows the power of his anger? " The mountains quake at him, and the hills melt, and the earth is burned at his presence, yea, the world, and all that dwell therein. Who can stand before his indignation? and who can abide in the fierceness of his anger? his fury is poured out like fire, and the rocks are thrown down by him," Nah. i. 5, 6.

His people know him, and have his dread upon them, by virtue whereof there is begot and maintained in them that godly awe and reverence of his majesty, which is agreeable to their profession of him. " Let him be your fear, and let him be your dread," Isa. viii. 13. Set his májesty before the eyes of your souls, and let his excellency make you afraid with godly fear.

There are these things that make God to be the fear of his people.

1. His presence is dreadful, and that not only his presence in common, but his special, yea, his most comfortable and joyous presence. When God comes to bring a soul news of mercy and salvation, even that visit, that presence of God is fearful. When Jacob went from Beer-sheba towards Haran, he met with God in the way, by a dream, in the which he saw a ladder set up on the earth, whose top reached to heaven; now, in this dream, from the top of this ladder, he saw the Lord, and heard him speak unto him, not threateningly, not as having his fury come up into his face; but in the most sweet and gracious manner, saluting him with promise of goodness after promise of goodness, to the number of eight or nine; as will appear if you read the place, Gen. xxviii. 10—17. Yet, I say, when he awoke, all the grace that discovered itself in this heavenly vision to him, could not keep him from dread and fear of God's majesty. "And Jacob awaked out of his sleep, and he said, Surely the Lord is in this place; and I knew it not. And he was afraid, and said, How dreadful is this place! this is none other but the house of God, and this is the gate of heaven."

At another time, to wit, when Jacob had that memorable visit from God, in which he gave him power as a prince to prevail with him; yea, and gave him a name, that by his remembering it he might call God's favour the better to his mind; yet even then and there, such dread of the majesty of God was upon him, that he went away wondering that his life was preserved, Gen. xxxii. 30. Man crumbles to dust at the presence of God; yea, though he shows himself to us in his robes of salvation.

We have read how dreadful and terrible even the presence of angels has been unto men, and that when they have brought them good tidings from heaven, Judges xiii. 22; Matt. xxviii. 5; Mark xvi. 5, 6.

Now, if angels, which are but creatures, are, through the glory that God has put upon them, so fearful and terrible in their appearance to men, how much more dreadful and terrible must God himself be to us, who are but dust and ashes! When Daniel had the vision of his salvation sent him from heaven, O Daniel, said the messenger, "a man greatly beloved;" yet behold the dread and terror of the person speaking fell with that weight upon this good man's soul, that he could not stand, nor bear up under it. He stood trembling, and cried out, "O my lord, by the vision my sorrows are turned upon me, and I have retained no strength. For how can the servant of this my lord talk with this my lord? for as for me, straightway there remained no strength in me," Dan. x. 16, 17.

See you here, if the presence of God is not a dreadful and a fearful thing, yea, his most gracious and merciful appearances; how much more then when he showeth himself to us as one that disliketh our ways, as one that is offended with us for our sins!

And there are three things that in an eminent manner make his presence dreadful to us.

(1.) The first is God's own greatness and majesty: the discovery of this, or of himself thus, even as no poor mortals are able to conceive of him, is altogether

unsupportable. The man dies to whom he thus
discovers himself. "And when I saw him," says
John, "I fell at his feet as dead," Rev. i. 17. It
was this, therefore, that Job would have avoided in the
day that he would have approached unto him. "Let
not thy dread," says he, "make me afraid. Then
call thou, and I will answer: or let me speak, and
answer thou me," Job xiii. 21, 22. But why doth
Job, after this manner, thus speak to God? why,
it was from a sense that he had of the dreadful
majesty of God, even the great and dreadful God
that keepeth covenant with his people.

The presence of a king is dreadful to the subject,
yea, though he carries it ever so condescendingly;
if then there be so much glory and dread in the
presence of a king, what fear and dread must there
be, think you, in the presence of the eternal God!

(2.) When God giveth his presence to his people,
that presence causeth them to appear to themselves
more what they are, than at other times, by all other
light they can see. "O my lord," said Daniel,
"by the vision my sorrows are turned upon me;"
and why was that, but because by the glory of that
vision, he saw his own vileness more than at other
times? So again; "I was left alone, and saw this
great vision;" and what follows? "and there remained no strength in me: for my comeliness was
turned in me into corruption, and I retained no
strength," Dan. x. 8. By the presence of God,
when we have it, indeed, even our best things, our
comeliness, our sanctity and righteousness, all do
immediately turn to corruption and polluted rags.
The brightness of his glory dims them, as the clear
light of the shining sun puts out the glory of the fire
or candle, and covers them with the shadow of death.

See also the truth of this in the vision of the prophet Isaiah. " Woe is me!" said he, " for I am undone; because I am a man of unclean lips, and I dwell in the midst of a people of unclean lips." Why, what is the matter? how came the prophet by this sight? he adds, " For mine eyes have seen the King, the Lord of hosts," Isa. vi. 5. But do you think that this outcry was caused by unbelief? no, nor yet begotten by slavish fear, this was to him the vision of his Saviour with whom also he had communion before. It was the glory of that God with whom he had now to do, that turned, as was noted before of Daniel, his comeliness in him into corruption, and that gave him yet greater sense of the disproportion that was betwixt his God and him, and so a greater sight of his defiled and polluted nature.

(3.) Add to this the revelation of God's goodness, and it must needs make his presence dreadful to us; for when a poor, defiled creature shall see, that this great God hath, notwithstanding his greatness, goodness in his heart, and mercy to bestow upon him; this makes his presence yet the more dreadful. They " shall fear the Lord and his goodness," Hos. iii. 5. The goodness as well as the greatness of God doth beget in the heart of his elect an awful reverence of his majesty. " Fear ye not me? saith the Lord: will ye not tremble at my presence?" and then to engage us in our soul to the duty, he adds one of his wonderful mercies to the world for a motive. Fear ye not me? why, who art thou? He answers, " which have placed the sand for the bound of the sea by a perpetual decree, that it cannot pass it: and though the waves thereof toss themselves, yet can they not prevail; though they roar, yet can they not pass over it," Jer. v. 22.

Also, when Job had God present with him, making manifest the goodness of his heart to him, what doth he say? how doth he behave himself in his presence? " I have heard of thee," says he, " by the hearing of the ear : but now mine eye seeth thee. Wherefore I abhor myself, and repent in dust and ashes," Job xlii. 5, 6.

And what mean the tremblings, the tears, the breakings and shakings of heart that attend the people of God, when in an eminent manner they receive the pronunciation of the forgiveness of sins at his mouth, but that the dread of the majesty of God is in their sight mixed therewith? God must appear like himself, speak to the soul like himself, nor can the sinner when under these glorious discoveries of its Lord and Saviour, keep out the beams of his majesty from the eyes of its understanding. " I will cleanse them," saith he, " from all their iniquity, whereby they have sinned against me ; and I will pardon all their iniquities, whereby they have sinned, and whereby they have transgressed against me." And what then ? " And they shall fear and tremble for all the goodness and for all the prosperity that I procure unto it," Jer. xxxiii. 8, 9.

Alas ! there is a company of poor, light, frothy professors in the world, that carry it under that which they call the presence of God, more like to antics than sober, sensible Christians ; yea, more like to fools than those that feel the presence of God. They would not carry it so in the presence of a king, nor yet of the lord of their land, were they but receivers of mercy at his hand : they carry it even in their most eminent seasons, as if the sense and sight of God, and his blessed grace to their souls in Christ, had a tendency in them to make men wanton : but,

THE FEAR OF GOD.

indeed, it is the most humbling and heart breaking sight in the world ; it is fearful.

Objection. But would you not have us rejoice at sight and sense of the forgiveness of our sins ?

Answer. Yes ; but yet I would have you, and indeed you shall, when God shall tell you that your sins are pardoned indeed, "rejoice with trembling," Psa. ii. 11. For then you have solid and godly joy ; a joyful heart, and wet eyes, in this will stand very well together, and it will be so more or less. For if God shall come to you, indeed, and visit you with the forgiveness of sins, that visit removeth the guilt, but increaseth the sense of thy filth ; and the sense of this, that God hath forgiven a filthy sinner, will make thee both rejoice and tremble. Oh the blessed confusion that will then cover thy face whilst thou, even thou, so vile a wretch shalt stand before God to receive at his hand thy pardon, and so the first fruits of thy eternal salvation ! "That thou mayest remember, and be confounded, and never open thy mouth any more because of thy shame, when I am pacified toward thee for all that thou hast done, saith the Lord God," Ezek. xvi. 63.

2. But as the presence, so the name of God is dreadful and fearful ; wherefore his name doth rightly go under the same title, "That thou mayest fear this glorious and fearful name, THE LORD THY GOD," Deut. xxviii. 58.

The name of God, what is that, but that by which he is distinguished and known from all others ? Names are to distinguish ; so man is distinguished from beasts, and angels from men ; so heaven from earth, and darkness from light ; especially when by the name, the nature of the thing is signified and expressed ; and so it was originally, for then names expressed the nature of the thing so named. And therefore it is that the name of God is the object of our fear, because by his name his nature is expressed. "Holy and reverend is his name," Psa. cxi. 9. And again proclaimed, "The Lord, the Lord God, merciful and gracious, long-suffering, and abundant in goodness and truth, keeping mercy for thousands, forgiving iniquity and transgression and sin, and that will by no means clear the guilty," Exod. xxxiv. 6, 7.

Also his names, "I am," Jah, Jehovah, with several others, what is by them intended, but that his nature, as his power, wisdom, eternity, goodness, and omnipotence, might be expressed and declared? The name of God is, therefore, the object of a Christian's fear. David prayed to God, "Unite my heart to fear thy name," Psa. lxxxvi. 11. Indeed, the name of God is a fearful name, and should always be reverenced by his people: yea, his name is to be feared for ever and ever, and that not only in his church and among his saints, but even in the world and among the heathen. "So the heathen shall fear the name of the Lord, and all the kings of the earth thy glory," Psa. cii. 15.

God tells us that his name is dreadful, and that he is pleased to see men afraid before his name, Mal. ii. 5. Yea, one reason why he executes so many judgments upon men as he doth, is that others might see, and fear his name. "So shall they fear the name of the Lord from the west, and his glory from the rising of the sun," Isa. lix. 19. "I gave them to him for the fear wherewith he feared me, and was afraid before my name," Mal. ii. 5.

The name of a king is a name of fear; and "I am a great King, saith the Lord of hosts," Mal.

i. 14. The name of master is a name of fear; "And if I be a Master, where is my fear, saith the Lord of hosts?" Mal. i. 6. Yea, rightly to fear the Lord, is a sign of a gracious heart. And again, "Unto you that fear my name," saith he, "shall the Sun of righteousness arise with healing in his wings;" yea, when Christ comes to judge the world. He will give reward to his servants the prophets, and to his saints, and to them that fear his name, small and great, Rev. xi. 18.

Now, I say, since the name of God is that by which his nature is expressed, and since he naturally is so glorious and incomprehensible, his name must needs be the object of our fear, and we ought always to have a reverential awe of God upon our hearts at what time soever we think of, or hear his name; but most of all, when we ourselves do take his holy and fearful name into our mouths, especially in a religious manner, that is, in preaching, praying, or holy conference. I do not by thus saying intend, as if it were lawful to make mention of his name in light and vain discourses; for we ought always to speak of it with reverence and godly fear; but I speak it to put Christians in mind that they should not in religious duties show lightness of mind, or be vain in their words, when yet they are making mention of the name of the Lord; and "let every one that nameth the name of Christ depart from iniquity," 2 Tim. ii. 19.

Make mention, then, of the name of the Lord at all times with great dread of his majesty upon your hearts, and in great soberness and truth. To do otherwise is to profane the name of the Lord, and to take his name in vain; and "the Lord will not hold him guiltless that taketh his name in vain," Exod.

xx. 7. Yea, God saith, that he will cut off the man
that doth it; so jealous is he of the honour due unto
his name, Lev. xx. 3.

This, therefore, showeth you the dreadful state of
those that lightly, vainly, lyingly, and profanely, make
use of the name, this fearful name of God ; either by
their blasphemous cursing and oaths, or by their
fraudulent dealing with their neighbour; but how
these men will escape, when they shall be judged,
devouring fire and everlasting burnings, for their
profaning and blaspheming of the name of the Lord,
it becomes them betimes to consider.

3. But as the presence and name of God are
dreadful and fearful in the church, so are his worship
and service. I say, his worship, or the works of service to which we are by him enjoined while we are
in this world, are dreadful and fearful things. This
David saith, "But as for me, I will come into thy
house in the multitude of thy mercy: and in thy
fear will I worship toward thy holy temple," Psa. v. 7.
And again, saith he, " Serve the Lord with fear,"
Psa. ii. 11.

To praise God is a part of his worship. But,
said Moses, "Who is like unto thee, O LORD,
among the gods? who is like thee, glorious in holiness, fearful in praises, doing wonders," Exod.
xv. 11. To rejoice before him is a part of his
worship; but David bids us " rejoice with trembling," Psa. ii. 11.

Yea, the whole of our service to God, and every
part thereof, ought to be done by us with reverence
and godly fear, Heb. xii. 28. And, therefore, let us,
as Paul saith again, " Cleanse ourselves from all filthiness of the flesh and spirit, perfecting holiness in
the fear of God," 2 Cor. vii. 1.

That which makes the worship of God so fearful a thing is,

(1.) For that it is the worship of God: all manner of service carries more or less dread and fear along with it, according as the quality or condition of the person is, to whom the worship and service are done. This is seen in the service of subjects to their princes, the service of servants to their lords, and the service of children to their parents. Divine worship then being due to God, and this God so great and dreadful in himself and name, his worship must, therefore, be a fearful thing.

(2.) Besides, this glorious Majesty is himself present to behold his worshippers in their worshiping him. "Where two or three are gathered together in my name, there am I in the midst of them," Matt. xviii. 20 ; that is, gathered together to worship him, I am there, saith he. And so, again, he is said to walk in the midst of the seven golden candlesticks, Rev. ii. 1 ; that is, in the churches ; and that with a countenance like the sun, with a head and hair as white as wool, and with eyes like .a flame of fire, Rev. i. 14—16. This puts dread and fear into his service ; and, therefore, his servants should serve him with fear.

(3.) Above all things, God is jealous of his worship and service. In all the ten commandments, he tells us not any thing of his being a jealous God, but in the second, which respects his worship. Look to yourselves, therefore, both as to the matter and manner of your worship ; " For I the Lord thy God," saith he, " am a jealous God, visiting the iniquity of the fathers upon the children," Exod. xx. 5. This, therefore, doth also put dread and fear into the worship and service of God.

c

(4.) The judgments that sometimes God hath executed upon men for their want of godly fear, while they have been in his worship and service, put fear and dread upon his holy appointments.

Nadab and Abihu were burned to death with fire from heaven; because they attempted to offer false fire upon God's altar, Lev. x. 1—3. And the reason rendered why they were so punished was, because God will be sanctified in those that come nigh him. To sanctify his name is to let him be thy dread and thy fear, and to do nothing in his worship but what is well pleasing to him. But because these men had not grace to do this, therefore they died before the Lord.

Eli's sons, for want of this fear, when they ministered in the holy worship of God, were both slain in one day by the sword of the uncircumcised Philistines, 1 Sam. iv. 11.

Uzza was smitten, and died before the Lord, for an unadvised touching the ark, when the men forsook it, 1 Chron. xiii. 9, 10.

Ananias, and Sapphira his wife, for telling a lie in the church when they were before God, were both stricken dead upon the place before them all, because they wanted the fear and dread of God's majesty, name, and service, when they came before him, Acts v. 1—10.

This, therefore, should teach us to conclude, that next to God's nature and name, his service, his instituted worship, is the most dreadful thing under heaven. His name is upon his ordinances, his eye is upon the worshippers, and his wrath and judgment upon those that worship not in his fear. For this cause some of those at Corinth were by God himself cut off, 1 Cor. xi. 30—32; and on others he has turned his back, and will again be with them no more.

This also rebuketh three sorts of people.

Such as regard not to worship God at all; be sure they have no reverence of his service, nor fear of his majesty before their eyes. Sinner, thou dost not come before the Lord to worship him; thou dost not bow before the high God; thou neither worshippest him in thy closet, nor in the congregation of saints. The fury of the Lord and his indignation must, in a short time, be poured out upon thee, and upon the families that call not upon his name, Psa. lxxix. 6; Jer. x. 25.

This rebukes such as count it enough to present their body in the place where God is worshipped, not minding with what heart, or with what spirit, they come thither. Some come into the worship of God to sleep there; some come thither to meet with their customers, and to get into the wicked fellowship of their vain companions; some come thither to feed their lustful and adulterous eyes with the flattering beauty of their fellow sinners. Oh, what a sad account will these worshippers give, when they shall account for all this, and be damned for it, because they came not to worship the Lord with that fear of his name that became them to come in, when they presented themselves before him!

This also rebukes those that care not so they worship, how, where, or after what manner they worship God. Those I mean, whose fear towards God is taught by the precepts of men. They are hypocrites; their worship also is vain, and a stench in the nostrils of God. Wherefore the Lord said, " Forasmuch as this people draw near me with their mouth, and with their lips do honour me, but

c 2

have removed their heart far from me, and their fear toward me is taught by the precept of men: therefore, behold, I will proceed to do a marvellous work among this people, even a marvellous work and a wonder: for the wisdom of their wise men shall perish, and the understanding of their prudent men shall be hid," Isa. xxix. 13, 14.

Thus I conclude this first thing, namely, that God is called our dread and fear.

CHAPTER II.

I SHALL now come to the second thing, to wit, the rule and directory of our fear.

Of this word FEAR, as it is taken for the word of God, the written word of God; for that also is, and ought to be, the rule and directory of our fear. So David calls it; "The fear of the Lord is clean, enduring for ever," Psa. xix. 9. The fear of the Lord, that is, the word of the Lord, the written word; for that which he calleth in this place the fear of the Lord, even in the same place he calleth the law, statutes, commandments, and judgments of God. "The law of the Lord is perfect, converting the soul: the testimony of the Lord is sure, making wise the simple. The statutes of the Lord are right, rejoicing the heart: the commandment of the Lord is pure, enlightening the eyes. The fear of the Lord is clean, enduring for ever: the judgments of the Lord are true and righteous altogether," ver. 7—9. All these words have respect to the same thing; to wit, the word of God, jointly designing the glory of it. Among which phrases, you see, this is one, "The fear of the Lord is clean, enduring for ever." This written word is, therefore, the object of a Christian's fear. This is that also which David intended when he said, "Come, ye children, hearken

c 3

unto me: I will teach you the fear of the Lord,"
Psa. xxxiv. 11.   I will teach you the fear, that is,
I will teach you the commandments, statutes, and
judgments of the Lord, even as Moses commanded
the children of Israel; "Thou shalt teach them
diligently unto thy children, and shalt talk of them
when thou sittest in thine house, and when thou
walkest by the way, and when thou liest down, and
when thou risest up," Deut. vi. 7.

That scripture also in Isaiah intends the same;
where the Father saith of the Son, that he shall be
" of quick understanding in the fear of the Lord;"
that he may " smite the earth with the rod of his
mouth," Isa. xi. 3, 4.   This rod in the text is none
other but the fear, the word of the Lord; for he
was to be of a quick understanding in it, that he
might smite, that is, execute it, according to the will
of his Father, upon and among the children of
men.

Now, this, as I said, is called the fear of the Lord,
because it is the rule and directory of our fear.   For
we know not how to fear the Lord in a saving way
without its guidance and direction.   As it is said of
the priest that was sent back from the captivity to
Samaria, to teach the people to fear the Lord; so it
is said concerning the written word, it is given to
us, and left among us, that we may read therein all
the days of our life, and learn to fear the Lord.   See
Deut. vi. 1—24; x. 12; xvii. 19.

And here it is that trembling at the word of God,
is even by God himself not only taken notice of, but
counted as laudable and praiseworthy, as is evident
in the case of Josiah, 2 Chron. xxxiv. 26, 27.

Such also are the approved of God, let them be

condemned by whomsoever they may. "Hear the word of the Lord, ye that tremble at his word; Your brethren that hated you, that cast you out for my name's sake, said, Let the Lord be glorified : but he shall appear to your joy, and they shall be ashamed," Isa. lxvi. 5.

Further, such shall be looked to by God himself, cared for and watched over, that no distress, temptation, or affliction, may overcome and destroy them. "To this man will I look," saith God, "even to him that is poor and of a contrite spirit, and trembleth at my word," Isa. lxvi. 2. It is the same in substance with that in the same prophet; "For thus saith the high and lofty One that inhabiteth eternity, whose name is Holy; I dwell in the high and holy place, with him also that is of a contrite and humble spirit, to revive the spirit of the humble, and to revive the heart of the contrite ones," Isa. lvii. 15. Yea, the way to escape dangers foretold is to hearken to, understand, and fear the word of God. "He that feared the word of the Lord among the servants of Pharaoh made his servants and his cattle flee into the houses : and he that regarded not the word of the Lord left his servants and his cattle in the field;" and they were destroyed of the hail, Exod. ix. 20—25.

If at any time the sins of a nation or church are discovered and bewailed, it is by those that know and tremble at the word of God. When Ezra heard of the wickedness of his brethren, and had a desire to humble himself before God for the same, who were those that assisted him in that matter, but those that trembled at the word of God? "Then," saith he, "were assembled unto me every one that trembled at the words of the God of Israel, because

of the transgression of those that had been carried
away," Ezra ix. 4.

Those also that tremble at the word are best able
to give counsel in the matters of God, for their judgment best suiteth with his mind and will.   "Now
therefore," said Shechaniah, " let us make a covenant
with our God to put away all the [strange] wives, and
such as are born of them, according to the counsel of
my lord, and of those that tremble at the commandment of our God ; and let it be done according to the
law," Ezra x. 3.

Now, something of the dread and terror of the
word lieth in these things.

1. As I have already hinted from the Author of
them ; they are the words of God.   Therefore you
have Moses and the prophets, when they come to
deliver their message to the people, still saying,
Hear the word of the Lord, Thus saith the Lord,
and the like.   So when Ezekiel was sent to the house
of Israel, in their state of religion, he was bid to say
unto them, " Thus saith the Lord God," Ezek. ii. 4 ;
iii. 11.

This is the honour and majesty, then, that God
hath put upon his written word ; and thus he hath
done, that we might make them the rule and directory of our fear, and that we might stand in awe
of, and tremble at them.   When Habakkuk heard
the word of the Lord, his belly trembled, and rottenness entered into his bones. " I trembled in myself,"
said he, " that I might rest in the day of trouble,"
Hab. iii. 16.   The word of a king is as the roaring of
a lion ; where the word of a king is, there is power,
Eccl. viii. 4 ; what is it, then, when God, the great
God, shall roar out of Zion, and utter his voice
from Jerusalem, whose voice shakes not only earth

but also heaven? How doth holy David set it forth;
" The voice of the Lord is powerful; the voice of
the Lord is full of majesty!" Psa. xxix. 4.

2. It is a word that is fearful, and may well be
called the fear of the Lord, because of the subject
matter of it; to wit, the state of sinners in another
world; for that is it unto which the whole Bible
bendeth itself, either more immediately, or more
mediately; all its doctrines, counsels, encourage-
ments, threatenings, and judgments, have a look one
way or other, upon us with respect to the next
world, which will be our last state, because it will be
to us an eternal state. This word, this law, these
judgments, are they that we shall be disposed of by.
" The word that I have spoken," said Christ, " the
same shall judge him in the last day," John xii. 48.
Now, if we consider that our next state must be
eternal, either eternal glory, or eternal fire, and that
this eternal glory, or this eternal fire must be our
portion according as the words of God, revealed in
the Holy Scriptures, shall determine; who will not
but conclude that, therefore, the words of God are
those at which we should tremble, and those by which
we should have our fear of God guided and directed, for by them we are taught how to please him
in every thing.

3. It is to be called a fearful word, because of the
truth and faithfulness of it. " The Scripture cannot be
broken," John x. 35. Hence it is called "the
Scripture of truth," Dan. x. 21; " the true sayings
of God," Rev. xix. 9; and also the fear of the Lord,
for that every jot and tittle thereof is for ever settled
in heaven, and stands more stedfast than doth the
world. " Heaven and earth," said Christ, " shall
pass away, but my word shall not pass away," Matt.

xxiv. 35. Those therefore that are favoured by the word of God, are favoured indeed, and that with the favour that no man can turn away; but those that by the word of the Scriptures are condemned, those can no man justify and set quit in the sight of God. Therefore what is bound by the text, is bound, and what is released by the text, is released; also the bond and release are unalterable. This therefore calleth upon God's people to stand more in fear of the word of God, than of all the terrors of the world.

There wanteth even in the hearts of God's people a greater reverence of the word of God, than to this day appears amongst us; and this let me say, that want of reverence of the word is the ground of all the disorders that are in the heart, life, conversation, and in Christian communion. Besides, the want of reverence of the word layeth men open to the fearful displeasure of God. "Whoso despiseth the word shall be destroyed: but he that feareth the commandment shall be rewarded," Prov. xiii. 13.

All transgression beginneth at wandering from the word of God; but, on the other side, David saith, "Concerning the works of men, by the word of thy lips I have kept me from the paths of the destroyer," Psa. xvii. 4. Therefore Solomon saith, "My son, attend to my words; incline thine ear unto my sayings. Let them not depart from thine eyes; keep them in the midst of thine heart. For they are life unto those that find them, and health to all their flesh," Prov. iv. 20—22.

Now, if indeed thou wouldst reverence the word of the Lord, and make it thy rule and directory in all things, believe that the word is the fear of the Lord; the word that standeth fast for ever: without and against which God will do nothing either in saving or condemning the souls of sinners.

But to conclude this, know, that those that have not due regard to the word of the Lord, and that make it not their dread and their fear, (but the rule of their life is the lusts of their flesh, and desire of their eyes, and the pride of life,) are sorely rebuked by this doctrine, and are counted the fools of the world; for " Lo, they have rejected the word of the Lord; and what wisdom is in them ?" Jer. viii. 9. That there are such people is evident, not only by their irregular lives, but by the manifest testimony of the word. "As for the word," said they to Jeremiah, "that thou hast spoken unto us in the name of the Lord, we will not hearken unto thee. But we will certainly do whatsoever thing goeth out of our own mouth," Jer. xliv. 16, 17.

Was this only the temper of wicked men then ? is not the same spirit of rebellion amongst us in our days? Doubtless there is, for there is no new thing: "The thing that hath been, it is that which shall be; and that which is done is that which shall be done: and there is no new thing under the sun," Eccles. i. 9.

Therefore as it was then, so it is with many in this day. As for the word of the Lord, it is nothing at all to them; their lusts, and whatever proceedeth out of their own mouths, that they will do, that they will follow. Now, such will certainly perish in their own rebellion; for this is as the sin of witchcraft; it was the sin of Korah and his company, and that which brought upon them such heavy judgments; yea, and they are made a sign that thou shouldst not do as they, for they perished, because they rejected the

word, the fear of the Lord, from among the congregation of the Lord, and they became a sign. The
word which thou despisest still abideth to denounce
its woe and judgment upon thee; and unless God
will save thee with the breath of his word, thou canst
never see his face with comfort.

Are the words of God called by the name of the
fear of the Lord? are they so dreadful in their re-
ceipt and sentence? then this rebukes those that
esteem the words and things of men more than the
words of God, as those do who are drawn from
their respect of, and obedience to, the word of God,
by the pleasures or threats of men.

Some there be who verily will acknowledge the
authority of the word, yet will not stoop their souls
thereto: such, whatever they think of themselves,
are judged by Christ to be ashamed of the word;
wherefore their state is damnable as the other.
"Whosoever," saith he, "shall be ashamed of me
and of my words in this adulterous and sinful generation, of him also shall the Son of man be ashamed,
when he cometh in the glory of his Father with the
holy angels," Mark viii. 38.

3. And if these things be so, what will become of
those that mock at, and professedly contemn, the
words of God, making them as a thing ridiculous,
and not to be regarded? Shall they prosper that do
such things? from the premises it is concluded that
their judgment now of a long time slumbereth not,
and when it comes it will devour them without
remedy. See 2 Chron. xxxvi. 15, 16.

If God, I say, hath put that reverence upon his
word, as to call it, the fear of the Lord, what will
become of those that do what they can to overthrow

its authority, by denying it to be his word, and by raising cavils against its authority? Such stumble indeed at the word, being appointed thereunto, but it shall judge them in the last day, 1 Pet. ii. 8; John xii. 48. But thus much for this.

Having thus spoken of the object and rule of our fear; I should come now to speak of fear, as it is a grace of the Spirit of God in the hearts of his people; but before I do that, I shall show you that there are divers sorts of fear besides. For man being a reasonable creature, and having even by nature a certain knowledge of God, hath also naturally something of some kind of fear of God at times, which although it be not that which is intended in the text, yet ought to be spoken to, that that which is not right, may be distinguished from that which is.

I will speak of several sorts of fear of God in the hearts of the children of men. There are, I say, several sorts or kinds of fear in the hearts of the sons of men; I mean, besides that fear of God which is intended in the text, and that accompanieth eternal life.

I shall here make mention of three of them.

1. There is a fear of God which flows from the light of nature.

2. There is a fear of God which flows from some of his dispensations to men, which yet is neither universal, nor saving.

3. There is a fear of God in the hearts of some men which is good and godly, but doth not for ever abide so.

To speak a little to all these, before I come to speak of fear as it is a grace of God in the hearts of his children.

D

1. And as to the first, to wit, that there is a fear of God which flows from the light of nature.

A people may be said to do things in a fear of God, when they act one towards another in things reasonable and honest betwixt man and man, not doing that to others they would not have done to themselves. This is that fear of God which Abraham thought the Philistines had destroyed in themselves, when he said of his wife to Abimelech, "She is my sister." For when Abimelech asked Abraham why he said of his wife, "She is my sister;" he replied, saying, "I thought, Surely the fear of God is not in this place; and they will slay me for my wife's sake," Gen. xx. 11. I thought, Verily that in this place men had stifled and choked that light of nature which is in them, at least so far as not to suffer it to put them in fear, when their lusts were powerful in them to accomplish their ends on the object that was present before them. But this I will pass by, and come to the second thing,

2. Namely, to show that there is a fear of God which flows from some of his dispensations to men, which yet is neither universal, nor saving. This fear when opposed to that which is saving, may be called an ungodly fear of God: I shall describe it by several particulars that follow.

(1.) There is a fear of God that causeth a continual grudging, discontent, and heart-risings against God, when under the hand of God; and that is, when the dread of God in his coming upon men to deal with them for their sins, is apprehended by them, and yet by this dispensation they have no change of heart to submit to him thereunder.

The sinners under this dispensation cannot shake

God out of their mind, nor yet graciously tremble before him, but through the unsanctified frame that they now are in, they are afraid with ungodly fear, and so in their minds are against him.

This fear oftentimes took hold of the children of Israel, when they were in the wilderness in their journey to the promised land; still they feared that God in this place would destroy them, but not with that fear that made them willing to submit, for their sins, to the judgment which they feared, but with that fear which made them oppose God.

This fear showed itself in them, even at the beginning of their journey, and was rebuked by Moses at the Red Sea; but it was not there, nor yet at any other place, so subdued, but that it would rise again in them at times to the dishonour of God, and make them anew guilty of sin before him. See Exod. xiv. 11, 12; Num. xiv. 1—10.

This fear is that which God said he would send before them in the day of Joshua, even a fear that should possess the inhabitants of the land; to wit, a fear that should arise for that faintness of heart that they should be swallowed up of, at their apprehending of Joshua in his approaches towards them to destroy them. "I will send my fear before thee, and will destroy all the people to whom thou shalt come, and I will make all thine enemies turn their backs unto thee," Exod. xxiii. 27. "This day," said God, "will I begin to put the dread of thee and the fear of thee upon the nations that are under the whole heavens, who shall hear report of thee, and shall tremble, and be in anguish because of thee," Deut. ii. 25.

Now, this fear is also, as you here see, called anguish, and in another place, a hornet; for it and

the soul that it falls upon, do greet each other as
boys and bees do.   The hornet puts men in fear, not
so as to bring the heart into a sweet compliance with
his terror, but so as to stir up the spirit into acts of
opposition and resistance, yet withal they flee before
it.   "I will send hornets before thee, which shall
drive out the Hivite, the Canaanite, and the Hittite,
from before thee," Exod. xxiii. 28.

Now, this fear, whether it be wrought by a mis-
apprehension of the judgments of God, as in the
Israelites, or otherwise, as in the Canaanites, yet un-
godliness is the effect thereof; and therefore I call it
an ungodly fear of God, for it stirreth up murmurings, discontents, and heart-risings against God,
while he with his dispensations is dealing with them.

(2.) There is a fear of God that driveth a man
away from God.   I speak not now of the atheist,
nor of the pleasurable sinner, nor yet of that fear
which I spake of just now; but I speak now of
such who through a sense of sin and of God's justice,
flee from him by a slavish, ungodly fear.   This ungodly fear was that which possessed Adam's heart
in the day that he did eat of the tree concerning
which the Lord had said unto him, "In the day that
thou eatest thereof thou shalt surely die," Gen.
ii. 17.   For then was he possessed with such a fear
of God as made him seek to hide himself from his
presence.   "I heard," said he, "thy voice in the
garden, and I was afraid, because I was naked; and I
hid myself," Gen. iii. 10.   Mind that, he had a fear
of God, but it was not godly; it was not that which
made him afterwards submit himself unto him; for
that would have kept him from departing from him,
or else have brought him to him again, with a bowed,
broken, and contrite spirit.   But this fear, as the

rest of his sin, managed his departing from his God, and pursued him to provoke him still so to do : by it he kept himself from God ; by it his whole man was carried away from him. I call it ungodly fear, because it begat in him ungodly apprehensions of his Maker ; because it confined Adam's conscience to the sense of justice only, and consequently to despair.

The same fear also possessed the children of Israel, when they heard the law delivered to them from Mount Sinai ; as is evident, for it made them that they could neither abide God's presence, nor hear his word. It drove them back from the mountain. It made them, saith the apostle to the Hebrews, that "they could not endure that which was commanded," Heb. xii. 20. Wherefore this fear Moses rebukes, and forbids their giving way thereto. "Fear not," said he ; but had that fear been godly, he would have encouraged it, and not have forbidden and rebuked it as he did. "Fear not," said he : "for God is come to prove you, and that his fear may be before your faces," Exod. xx. 20. Therefore, that fear which already had taken possession of them, was not the fear of God, but a fear that was of Satan, of their own misjudging hearts, and so a fear that was ungodly. Mark you, here is a fear and a fear ; a fear forbidden, and a fear commended : a fear forbidden, because it engendered their hearts to bondage, and to ungodly thoughts of God and of his word ; it made them that they could not desire to "hear God speak to them any more," ver. 19.

Many also at this day are possessed with this ungodly fear ; and you may know them by this :— they cannot abide conviction for sin ; and if at any time the word of the law, by the preaching of the word, comes near them, they will not abide that preacher, nor such kind of sermons any more. They are, as they deem, best at ease when furthest off from God and of the power of his word. The word preached brings God nearer to them than they desire he should come, because, whenever God comes near, their sins by him are manifest, and so is the judgment that to them is due. Now, these not having faith in the mercy of God through Christ, nor that grace that tendeth to bring them to him, they cannot but think of God amiss; and their so thinking of him makes them say unto God, "Depart from us; for we desire not the knowledge of thy ways," Job xxi. 14. Wherefore, their wrong thoughts of God beget in them this ungodly fear: and again, this ungodly fear doth maintain in them the continuance of these wrong and unworthy thoughts of God; and, therefore, through that devilish service wherewith they strengthen one another, the sinner, without a miracle of grace prevents him, is drowned in destruction and perdition.

It was this ungodly fear of God that carried Cain from the presence of God into the land of Nod, and that put him there upon any carnal worldly business, if, perhaps, he might by so doing stifle convictions of the majesty and justice of God against his sin, and so live the rest of his vain life in the more sinful security and fleshly ease.

This ungodly fear is that also which Samuel perceived at the people's apprehension of their sin, to begin to get hold of their hearts; wherefore he, as Moses before him, quickly forbids their entertaining of it. "Fear not," said he: "ye have done all this wickedness: yet turn not aside from following the Lord," 1 Sam. xii. 20. For to turn them aside

THE FEAR OF GOD.

from following of him, was the natural tendency of this fear. But fear not, said he, that is, with that fear that tendeth to turn you aside. Now, I say, 'the matter that this fear worketh upon (as in Adam, and the Israelites, mentioned before) was their sin. You have sinned, said he, that is true, yet turn not aside; yet fear not with that fear that would make you so do. Note by the way, sinner, that when the greatness of thy sins, being apprehended by thee, shall work in thee that fear of God as shall incline thy heart to flee from him, thou art possessed with a fear of God that is ungodly, yea, so ungodly, that not any of thy sins for heinousness may be compared therewith, (as might be made manifest in many particulars;) but Samuel having rebuked this fear, presently set before the people another, to wit, the true fear of God; "Fear the Lord," said he, "and serve him in truth with all your heart," ver. 24; and he giveth them this encouragement so to do, "for the Lord will not forsake his people," ver. 22.

This ungodly fear is that which you read of in many other places; and God's people should shun it as they would shun the devil, because its natural tendency is to forward the destruction of the soul in which it has taken possession.

(3.) There is a fear of God, which, although it hath not in it that power as to make men flee from God's presence, yet it is ungodly, because, even while they are in the outward way of God's ordinances, their hearts are by it quite discouraged from attempting to exercise themselves in the power of religion.

Of this sort are those that dare not cast off the hearing, reading, and discoursing of the word, as others : no, nor the assembly of God's children for

the exercise of other religious duties, for their conscience is convinced this is the way and worship
of God. But yet their heart by this ungodly
fear, is kept from a powerful, gracious falling in
with God. This fear takes away their heart from
all holy and godly prayer in private, and from all holy
and godly zeal for his name in public; and there be
many professors whose hearts are possessed with this
ungodly fear of God; and they are intended by the
slothful servant. He was a servant, a servant among
the servants of God, and had gifts and abilities given
him, therewith to serve Christ, as well as his fellows,
yea, and was commanded too, as well as the rest, to
occupy till his master came. But what does he?
why, he takes his talent, the gift that he was to lay
out for his master's profit, and puts it in a napkin;
digs a hole in the earth, and hides his Lord's money,
and lies at a lazy manner all his days, not out of,
but in his Lord's vineyard; for he came among the
servants also at last. By which it is manifest, that
he had not cast off his profession, but was slothful
and negligent while he was in it. But what was it
that made him thus slothful? what was it that took
away his heart while he was in the way, and that
discouraged him from falling in with the power and
holy practice of religion according to the talent he
received? Why, it was this, he gave way to an ungodly fear of God, and that took away his heart from
the power of religious duties. "Lord," said he,
"behold, here is thy pound, which I have kept laid
up in a napkin: for I feared thee." Why, man,
doth the fear of God make a man idle and slothful?
No, no; that is, if it be right and godly. This fear
was, therefore, evil fear; it was that ungodly fear of
God, of which I have here been speaking of. "For

I feared thee," or as Matthew hath it, "for I was afraid." Afraid of what? of Christ, that he was an hard man, reaping where he sowed not, and gathering where he had not strewed? This his fear, being ungodly, made him apprehend of Christ contrary to the goodness of his nature, and so took away his heart from all endeavours to be doing of that which was pleasing in his sight, Luke xix. 20—26; Matt. xxv. 24—30.

And thus do all those that retain the name and show of religion, but are neglecters as to the power and godly practice of it. These will live like dogs and swine in the house. They pray not, they watch not their hearts, they pull not their hands out of their bosoms to work, they do not strive against their lusts, nor will they ever resist unto blood, striving against sin; they will not take up their cross, or improve what they have to God's glory.

Let all men, therefore, take heed of this ungodly fear, and shun it, for it will make them afraid where no fear is. It will tell them that there is a lion in the street; the unlikeliest place in the world for such a beast to be in : it will put a mask upon the face of God, most dreadful and fearful to behold, and then quite discourage the soul as to his service. So it served the slothful servant, and so it will serve thee, poor sinner, if thou entertainest it, and givest way thereto.

(4.) This ungodly fear of God shows itself also in this :—it will not suffer the soul that is governed thereby to trust only to Christ for justification of life, but will bend the powers of the soul to trust partly to the works of the law. Many of the Jews were, in the time of Christ and his apostles, possessed with this ungodly fear of God; for they

were not as the former, namely, as the slothful servant, to receive a talent, and hide it in the earth in a
napkin, but they were an industrious people, "which
followed after the law of righteousness," Rom.
ix. 31; they had a zeal of God, and of the religion of
their fathers, but how then did they come to mis-
carry? Why, their fear of God was ungodly; it
would not suffer them wholly to trust to the righteousness of faith, which is the imputed righteousness
of Christ. They "followed after the law of righteousness," but attained not to the law of righteousness.
"Wherefore? Because they sought it not by faith,
but as it were by the works of the law," ver. 32.
But what was it that made them join their works of
the law with Christ, but their unbelief, whose foundation was ignorance and fear: they were afraid to
venture all in one bottom, they thought two strings
to one bow would be best, and thus betwixt two
stools they came to the ground. And hence, to fear
and to doubt are put together, as being the cause one
of another; yea, they are put ofttimes the one for
the other: thus, ungodly fear for unbelief; "Be not
afraid, only believe," Mark v. 36; and, therefore,
he that is over-ruled and carried away with this fear,
is coupled with the unbeliever that is thrust out from
the holy city among the dogs. But the fearful, and
unbelievers, and murderers, are without, Rev. xxi. 8.
The fearful and unbelieving, you see, are put together,
for, indeed, fear, that is, this ungodly fear, is the
ground of unbelief; or, if you will, unbelief is the
ground of this fear: but I stand not upon nice
distinctions. This ungodly fear hath a great hand
in keeping of the soul from trusting only to Christ's
righteousness for justification of life.

(5.) This ungodly fear of God is that which

will put men upon adding to the revealed will of
God, their own inventions, and their own performances of them, as a means to pacify the anger of
God. For the truth is, where this ungodly fear
reigneth, there is no end of law and duty. When
those people that you read of in 2 Kings xvii. 26,
were destroyed by the lions, because they had set
up idolatry in the land of Israel, they sent for, a
priest from Babylon that might teach them the
manner of the God of the land: but, behold, when
they knew it, being taught it by the priest, yet their
fear would not suffer them to be content with that
worship only. "They feared the Lord, and served
their own gods," ver. 33. And, again, "So these
nations feared the Lord, and served their graven
images," ver. 41. It was this fear also that put
the Pharisees upon inventing so many traditions as
the washing of cups, pots, brazen vessels and tables,
with abundance of such other like things, Mark
vii. 4. None knows the many dangers that an ungodly fear of God will drive a man into. How has
it racked and tortured the papists for hundreds of
years together! For what else is the cause but this
ungodly fear, at least in the most simple and harm-
less of them, of their penances, as creeping to the
cross, going barefoot on pilgrimage, whipping themselves, wearing of sackcloth, saying so many pater-
nosters, so many ave-marias, making so many confessions to the priest, giving so much money for
pardons, and abundance of other the like, but this
ungodly fear of God? For, could they be brought
to believe this doctrine, that Christ "was delivered
for our offences, and was raised again for our justification," Rom. iv. 25, and to apply it by faith with
godly boldness to their own souls, this fear would

vanish, and so consequently all those things with
which they so needlessly and unprofitably afflict
themselves, are very offensive to God, and grieve
his people.

Therefore, gentle reader, although my text doth
indeed bid that thou shouldst fear God; yet it in-
cludeth not, nor accepteth of *any* fear; no, not of
any fear of God. For there is, as you see, a fear of
God that is ungodly, and that is to be shunned as
other sins. Wherefore, thy wisdom and thy care
should be, to see and prove thy fear to be godly,
which shall be the next thing that I shall take in
hand.

3. The third thing that I am to speak to is, that
there is a fear of God in the hearts of some men that
is good and godly, but yet doth not for ever abide so.
Or you may take it thus:—there is a fear of God,
that is godly but for a time.

In my speaking to, and opening of this to you, I
shall observe this method :

(1.) I shall show you what this fear is.

(2.) I shall show you by whom, or by what, this
fear is wrought in the heart.

(3.) I shall show you what this fear doth in the
soul.

(1.) For the first, this fear is an effect of sound
awakenings by the word of wrath, which begetteth in
the soul a sense of its right to eternal damnation ;
for this fear is not in every sinner. He that is blinded
by the devil, and that is not able to see that his state
is damnable, hath not this fear in his heart ; but
he that is under the powerful workings of the word
of wrath, as God's elect are at first conversion, he
hath this godly fear in his heart ; that is, he fears

that that damnation will come upon him, which by the justice of God is due unto him, because he has broken his holy law. This is the fear that made the three thousand cry out, "Men and brethren, what shall we do?" Acts ii. 37 ; and that made the jailor cry out, and that with great trembling of soul, " Sirs, what must I do to be saved ?" Acts xvi. 30.

The method of God is to kill, and then make alive ; to smite, and then heal. When the commandment came to Paul, sin revived, and he died; and that law which was ordained to life, he found to be unto death, Rom. vii. 9, 10. That is, it passed a sentence of death upon him for his sins, and slew his conscience with that sentence. Therefore from that time that he heard that word, Why dost thou persecute me? which is all one, as if he had said, Why dost thou commit murder? he lay under the sentence of condemnation by the law, and under this fear of that sentence in his conscience. He lay, I say, under it, until Ananias came to him to comfort him, and to preach unto him the forgiveness of sins, Acts ix. 17.

The fear, therefore, that now I call godly, is that fear which is properly called the fear of eternal damnation for sin ; and this fear at first awakening, is good and godly, because it ariseth in the soul from a true sense of its very state. Its state by nature is damnable, because it is sinful, and because he is not one that as yet believeth in Christ for remission of sins. "He that believeth not shall be damned," Mark xvi. 16. " He that believeth not is condemned already," and " the wrath of God abideth on him," John iii. 18, 36. The which, when the sinner at first begins to see, he justly fears it; I say, he fears it justly, and therefore godly, because

E

by this fear he subscribes to the sentence that is gone
out against him for sin.

(2.) We now inquire, By whom, or by what, is
this fear wrought in the heart?

To this I shall answer in brief. It is wrought in
the heart by the Spirit of God, working there at first
as a Spirit of bondage, on purpose to put us in fear.
This Paul teacheth in Rom. viii. 15, saying, "Ye
have not received the spirit of bondage again to fear."
He doth not say, Ye have not received the Spirit of
bondage; for that they had received, and that to put
them in fear, which was at first conversion, as by
the instances made mention of before is manifest:
all that he says is, that they had not received it
again; that is, after the Spirit, as a Spirit of adoption
is come; for then, as a spirit of bondage it cometh
no more.

It is then the Spirit of God, even the Holy Ghost,
that convinceth us of sin, and so of our damnable
state, because of sin, John xvi. 8, 9. For it cannot
be that the Spirit of God should convince us of sin,
but it must also show us our state to be damnable
because of it; especially if it so convinceth us, before
we believe, and that is the intent of our Lord in that
place, " of sin," (and so of their damnable state by
sin,) "because they believe not on me." Therefore,
the Spirit of God, when he worketh in the heart, as
a Spirit of bondage, he doth it by working in us by
the law; " for by the law is the knowledge of sin,"
Rom. iii. 20. And he, in this his working, is properly called a Spirit of bondage.

[1.] Because, by the law he shows us, that indeed
we are in bondage to the law, the devil, death,
and damnation; for this is our proper state by

nature, though we see it not until the Spirit of God shall come to reveal this our state of bondage unto our own senses by revealing to us our sins by the law.

[2.] He is called, in this his working, the Spirit of bondage, because he here also holds us, to wit, in this sight and sense of our bondage-state, so long as is meet we should be so held, which to some of the saints is a longer, and to some a shorter time. Paul was held in it three days and three nights, but the jailor and the three thousand, so far as can be gathered, not above an hour; but some in these later times are so held for days and months, if not years.

But I say, let the time be longer or shorter, it is the Spirit of God that holdeth him under this yoke; and it is good that a man should be his time held under it; as is that saying of the Lamentations: "It is good for a man that he bear the yoke in his youth," Lam. iii. 27; that is, at his first awakening. So long as seems good to this Holy Spirit to work in this manner by the law.

Now, as I said, the sinner at first is by the Spirit of God held in this bondage; that is, hath such a discovery of his sin, and of his damnation for sin, made to him, and also is held so fast under the sense thereof, that it is not in the power of any man, nor yet of the very angels in heaven, to release him, or set him free, until the Holy Spirit changeth his ministration, and comes in the sweet and peaceable tidings of salvation by Christ in the gospel, to his poor, dejected, and afflicted conscience.

(3.) I now come to show you what this fear does in the soul.

Now, although this godly fear is not to last always with us, yet it greatly differs from that which is wholly ungodly of itself, both because of the author, and also of the effects of it. Of the author I have told you before, I now shall tell you what it doth.

[1.] This fear makes a man judge himself for sin, and to fall down before God with a broken heart under this judgment: the which is pleasing to God, because the sinner, by so doing, justifies God in his saying, and clears him in his judgment.

[2.] As this fear makes a man judge himself, and cast himself down at God's footstool, so it makes him condole and bewail his misery before him, which is also well pleasing in his sight. "I have surely heard Ephraim bemoaning himself thus; Thou hast chastised me, and I was chastised, as a bullock unaccustomed to the yoke: turn thou me, and I shall be turned; for thou art the Lord my God. Surely after that I was turned, I repented; and after that I was instructed, I smote upon my thigh: I was ashamed, yea, even confounded, because I did bear the reproach of my youth," Jer. xxxi. 18, 19.

[3.] This fear makes a man lie at God's footstool, and puts his mouth in the dust, if so be there may be hope. This also is well pleasing to God, because now is the sinner as nothing, and in his own eyes less than nothing, as to any good or desert. "He sitteth alone and keepeth silence, because he hath borne it upon him. He putteth his mouth in the dust; if so be there may be hope," Lam. iii. 28, 29.

[4.] This fear puts a man upon crying to God for mercy, and that in a most humble manner: now he sensibly cries, now he dejectedly cries, now he feels and cries, now he smarts and cries out, "God be merciful to me a sinner," Luke xviii. 13.

[5.] This fear makes a man that he cannot accept of that for support and succour, which others that are destitute thereof will take up and be contented with. This man must be washed by God himself, and cleansed from his sin by God himself. See Psa. li.

[6.] Therefore, this fear goes not away until the Spirit of God changes his ministration as to this particular, in leaving off to work now by the law, as before, and coming to the soul with the sweet word of promise of life and salvation by Jesus Christ.

Thus far this fear is godly ; that is, until Christ, by the Spirit in the gospel, is revealed and made over unto us ; and no longer. Thus far this fear is godly, and the reason why it is godly, is because the ground-work of it is good. I told you before what this fear is, namely, it is the fear of damnation. Now, the ground for this fear is good, as is manifest, by these particulars.

The soul feareth damnation, and that rightly, because it is in its sins.

Again ; The soul feareth damnation rightly, because it hath not faith in Christ, but is at present under the law.

Further ; The soul feareth damnation rightly, because by sin, the law, and for want of faith, the wrath of God, abideth on it.

But now, although thus far this fear of God is good and godly, yet after Christ, by the Spirit in the word of the gospel, is revealed to us, and we made to accept of him as so revealed and offered to us, by a true and living faith, this fear, to wit, of damnation, is no longer good, but ungodly. Nor doth the Spirit of God ever work it in us again ; " For ye have not received the Spirit of bondage again to fear," that is to say, to fear damnation ; " but ye have received the Spirit of adoption, whereby we cry, Abba, Father," Rom. viii. 15.

But I would not be mistaken, when I say, that

this fear is no longer godly. I do not mean with
reference to the essence and habit of it; for I believe
it is the same in the seed, which shall afterwards
grow up to an higher degree, and into a more sweet
and gospel current, and manner of working; but I
mean with reference to this act of fearing damnation:
I say, it shall never by the Spirit be managed to that
work, it shall never bring forth that fruit more.

And my reasons are,—

[1.] Because that the soul, by closing through the
promise, by the Spirit, with Jesus Christ, is removed
off that foundation upon which it stood, when it justly
feared damnation: it hath received now forgiveness
of sin; it is now no more under the law, but in Jesus
Christ by faith; therefore, there is now no condemnation to it, Rom. viii. 1. The groundwork therefore
being now taken away, the Spirit worketh that fear
no more.

[2.] He cannot, after he hath come to the soul as a
Spirit of adoption, come again as a Spirit of bondage,
to put the soul into its first fear, to wit, a fear of
eternal damnation, because he cannot say and unsay,
do and undo. As a Spirit of adoption he told me
that my sins were forgiven me, that I was included
in the covenant of grace, that God was my Father
through Christ, that I was under the promise of
salvation, and that this calling and gift of God to me
is permanent, and without repentance. And do you
think, that after he hath told me this, and sealed up
the truth of it to my precious soul, that he will come
to me, and tell me that I am yet in my sins, under
the curse of the law and the eternal wrath of God?
No, no; the word of the gospel is not yea, yea; nay,
nay: it is only yea, and amen; it is so, as God is
true, 2 Cor. i. 17, 20.

[3.] The state, therefore, of the sinner being changed, and that too by the Spirit's changing his dispensation, leaving off to be now a Spirit of bondage to put us in fear, and coming to our heart as the Spirit of adoption, to make us cry, Father, Father, he cannot go back to his first work again; for if so, then he must gratify, yea and also ratify, that profane and popish doctrine, forgiven to-day, unforgiven to-morrow; a child of God to-day, a child of hell to-morrow. But what saith the Scriptures? " Now therefore ye are no more strangers and foreigners, but fellow citizens with the saints, and of the household of God; and are built upon the foundation of the apostles and prophets, Jesus Christ himself being the chief corner stone; in whom all the building fitly framed together groweth unto an holy temple in the Lord: in whom ye also are builded together for an habitation of God through the Spirit," Eph. ii. 19—22.

Object. But this is contrary to my experience.

Why, Christian, what is thy experience?

Why, I was at first, as you have said, possessed with the fear of damnation, and so under the power of the Spirit of bondage.

Well said, and how was it then?

Why, after some time of continuance in these fears, I had the Spirit of adoption sent to me to seal up to my soul the forgiveness of sins; and so he did: and was also helped by the same Spirit, as you have said, to call God, Father, Father.

Well said, and what after that?

Why, after that I fell into as great fears as ever I was in before.

Ans. All this may be granted, and yet nevertheless, what I have said will abide a truth; for I have

not said that after the Spirit of adoption is come, a
Christian shall not again be in as great fears, for he
may have worse than he had at first; but I say, that
after the Spirit of adoption is come, the Spirit of
bondage, as such, is sent of God no more to put us
into those fears. For, mark, " For we have not received the Spirit of bondage again to fear." Let the
word be true, whatever thy experience is. Dost thou
not understand me ?

After the Spirit of God has told me, and also
helped me to believe it, that the Lord, for Christ's
sake, hath forgiven mine iniquities; he tells me no
more, that they are not forgiven. After the Spirit
of God has helped me, through Christ, to call God
my Father, he tells me no more that the devil is my
father. After he hath told me, that I am not under
the law, but under grace, he tells me no more that I
am not under grace, but under the law, and bound
over by it, for my sins, to the wrath and judgment
of God : but this is the fear that the Spirit as the
Spirit of bondage worketh in the soul at first.

Quest. Can you give me further reason yet to
convince me of the truth of what you say?

Ans. 1. Yes, because, as the Spirit cannot give
himself the lie, so he cannot overthrow his own
order of working, nor yet contradict that testimony
that his servants, by his inspiration, have given. of
his order of working with them.

But he must do the first, if he saith to us, and
that after we have received his own testimony that
we are under grace, that yet we are under sin, the
law, and wrath.

And he must do the second, if, after he hath gone
through the first work on us, as a Spirit of bondage,
to the second as a Spirit of adoption; he should

overthrow as a Spirit of bondage again, what before he had built as a Spirit of adoption.

And the third must therefore needs follow; that is, he overthroweth the testimony of his servants; for they have said, that now we receive the Spirit of bondage again to fear no more; that is, after that we, by the Holy Ghost, are enabled to call God, Father, Father.

Ans. 2. This is evident, also, because the covenant abideth in which the soul is now interested, and is everlasting; not upon the supposition of my obedience, but upon the unchangeable purpose of God, and the efficacy of the obedience of Christ, whose blood also hath confirmed it. It is "ordered in all things, and sure," said David; "for this," added he, "is all my salvation," 2 Sam. xxiii. 5.

The covenant, then, is everlasting in itself, being established upon so good a foundation, and therefore standeth in itself everlastingly bent for the good of those that are involved in it. Hear the tenor of the covenant, and God's attesting of the truth thereof. " This is the covenant that I will make with the house of Israel after those days, saith the Lord; I will put my laws into their mind, and write them in their hearts: and I will be to them a God, and they shall be to me a people: and they shall not teach every man his neighbour, and every man his brother, saying, Know the Lord: for all shall know me, from the least to the greatest. For I will be merciful to their unrighteousness, and their sins and their iniquities will I remember no more," Heb. viii. 10— 12. Now, if God will do thus unto those that he hath comprised in his everlasting covenant of grace, then he will remember their sins no more; that is, unto condemnation; for so it is, that he doth forget them:

then cannot the Holy Ghost, who also is one with the Father and the Son, come to us again, even after we are possessed with these glorious fruits of this covenant, as a Spirit of bondage, to put us in fear of damnation.

Ans. 3. The Spirit of God, after it is come to me as a Spirit of adoption, can come to me no more as a Spirit of bondage, to put me in fear, that is, with my first fear; because, by that faith that he, even he himself, hath wrought in me, to believe and call God, Father, Father, I am united to Christ, and stand no more in my own sins or performances; but in his glorious righteousness before him, and before his Father; and he will not cast away a member of his body, of his flesh, and of his bones. Nor will the Spirit of God come as a Spirit of bondage, to put me into a grounded fear of damnation, that standeth complete before God in the righteousness of Christ; for that is an apparent contradiction.

Quest. But may he not come again as a Spirit of bondage, to put me into my first fears for my good?

Ans. The text saith the contrary; " For we have not received the Spirit of bondage again to fear." Nor is God put to it for want of wisdom, to say and unsay, do and undo, or else he cannot do good. When we are sons, and have received the adoption of children, he doth not use to send the Spirit after that to tell us we are slaves and heirs of damnation, that we are without Christ, without the promise, without grace, and without God in the world; and yet this he must do, if the Spirit comes to us after we have received him as a Spirit of adoption, and put us, as a Spirit of bondage, in fear as before.

Quest. But by what spirit is it, then, that I am

brought again into fears, even into the fears of damnation, and so into bondage?

Ans. By the spirit of the devil, who always labours to frustrate the faith, and hope, and comfort of the godly.

Quest. How doth that appear?

Ans. By the groundlessness of such fears—by the unseasonableness of them—and by the effects of them.

By the *groundlessness* of such fears. The ground is removed; for a grounded fear of damnation is this; I am yet in my sins, in a state of nature, under the law, without faith, and so under the wrath of God. This, I say, is the ground of the fear of damnation, the true ground to fear it; but now, the man that we are talking of, is one that hath the ground of this fear taken away, by the testimony and seal of the Spirit of adoption: he is said to be justified; and has, for the truth of this his condition, received the evidence of the Spirit of adoption, and hath been thereby enabled to call God, Father, Father. Now, he that hath received this, has the ground of the fear of damnation taken from him; therefore his fear, I say, being without ground, is false, and so no work of the Spirit of God.

By the *unseasonableness* of them. This spirit always comes too late. It comes after the Spirit of adoption is come. Satan is always too soon, or too late. If he would have men believe they are children, he would have them believe it while they are slaves, slaves to him and their lusts. If he would have them believe they are slaves, it is when they are sons, and have received the Spirit of adoption, and the testimony, by that, of their sonship before. And this evil is rooted even in his nature; he is a liar, and the father of it, John viii. 44 ; and his lies are not more known to saints than in this, that he labours always to contradict the work and order of the Spirit of truth.

It also appears by the *effects* of such fears. For there is a great deal of difference betwixt the natural effects of these fears, which are wrought indeed by the Spirit of bondage, and those which are wrought by this spirit of the devil afterwards.

The one, to wit, the fears that are wrought by the Spirit of bondage, causeth us to confess the truth, that we are Christless, graceless, faithless, and so at present, that is, while he is so working, in a sinful and damnable case ; but the spirit of the devil, when he comes, which is after the Spirit of adoption is come, he causeth us to make a lie, that is to say, we are Christless, graceless, and faithless. Now, this I say is wholly, and in all the parts of it, a lie, and he is the father of it.

Besides the direct tendency of the fear that the Spirit of God, as a Spirit of bondage, worketh in the soul, is to cause us to come repenting home to God by Jesus Christ ; but these latter fears tend directly to make a man, (he having first denied the work of God, as he will, if he falleth in with these fears,) to run quite away from God, and from his grace to him in Christ, as will evidently appear if thou givest but a plain and honest answer to these following questions.

Quest. 1. Do not these fears make thee question, whether there was ever a work of grace wrought in thy soul?

Ans. Yes, verily, that they do.

Quest. 2. Do not these fears make thee question, whether ever thy first fears were wrought by the Holy Spirit of God?

Ans. Yes, verily, that they do.

Quest. 3. Do not these fears make thee question, whether ever thou hast had indeed any true comfort from the word and Spirit of God?

Ans. Yes, verily, that they do.

Quest. 4. Dost thou not find intermixed with these fears, plain assertions that thy first comforts were either from thy fancy, or from the devil, and a fruit of his delusions?

Ans. Yes, verily, that I do.

Quest. 5. Do not these fears weaken thy heart in prayer?

Ans. Yes, that they do.

Quest. 6. Do not these fears keep thee back from laying hold of the promise of salvation by Jesus Christ?

Ans. Yes; for I think if I were deceived before, if I were comforted by a spirit of delusion before; why may it not be so again: so I am afraid to take hold of the promise.

Quest. 7. Do not these fears tend to the hardening of thy heart, and to the making of thee desperate?

Ans. Yes, verily, that they do.

Quest. 8. Do not these fears hinder thee from profiting in hearing or reading of the word?

Ans. Yes, verily, for still whatever I hear or read, I think nothing that is good belongs to me.

Quest. 9. Do not these fears tend to the stirring up of blasphemies in thy heart against God?

Ans. Yes, to the almost distracting of me.

Quest. 10. Do not these fears make thee sometimes think, that it is in vain for thee to wait upon the Lord any longer?

Ans. Yes, verily; and I have many times almost come to this conclusion, that I will read, pray, hear, company with God's people, or the like, no longer.

Well, poor Christian, I am glad that thou hast so plainly answered me; but, I pray thee, look back upon thy answer, how much of God, dost thou think, is in these things? how much of his Spirit, and the grace of his word? Just none at all; for it cannot be that these things can be the true and natural effects of the workings of the Spirit of God; no, not as a Spirit of bondage. These are not his doings; dost thou not see the very paw of the devil in them? yea, in every one of thy ten confessions? Is there not palpably high wickedness in every one of the effects of this fear?

I conclude then, as I began, that the fear that the Spirit of God, as a Spirit of bondage, worketh, is good and godly, not only because of the Author, but also because of the ground and effects; but yet it can last no longer as such, as producing the aforesaid conclusion, than till the Spirit, as the Spirit of adoption comes; because that then the soul is manifestly taken out of the state and condition into which it had brought itself by nature and sin, and is put into Christ, and so by him into a state of life and blessedness by grace. Therefore, if first fears come again into thy soul after that the Spirit of adoption hath been with thee, know they come not from the Spirit of God, but from the spirit of the devil, for they are a lie in themselves, and their effects are sinful and devilish.

Object. But I had also such wickedness as that in my heart at my first awaking, and therefore, by your argument, neither should that be but from the devil.

Ans. So far forth as such wickedness was in thy heart, so far did the devil and thine own heart seek to drive thee to despair, and drown thee there; but thou hast forgot the question: the question is not whether then thou wert troubled with such iniquities, but whether thy fears of damnation at that time were not just and good, because grounded upon thy present condition, which was, for that thou wast out of Christ, in thy sins, and under the curse of the law; and whether now, since the Spirit of adoption is come unto thee, and hath thee, and hath done that for thee as hath been mentioned, I say, whether thou oughtest for any thing whatever to give way to the same fear, from the same ground of damnation; it is evident thou oughtest not, because the ground, the cause is removed.

Object. But since I was sealed to the day of redemption, I have grievously sinned against God; have not I therefore cause to fear, as before? May not therefore the Spirit of bondage be sent again to put me in fear as at first? Sin was the first cause, and I have sinned now.

Ans. No, by no means; "for we have not received the Spirit of bondage again to fear." That is, God hath not given it us, "for God hath not given us the spirit of fear; but of power, and of love, and of a sound mind," 2 Tim. i. 7.

If, therefore, our first fears come upon us again, after that we have received at God's hands the spirit of love, of power, and of a sound mind, they are to be refused, though we have grievously sinned against our God. This is manifest from 1 Sam. xii. 20; "Fear not: ye have done all this wickedness." That is, not with that fear which would have made them flee from God, as concluding that they were not now his people.

And the reason is, because sin cannot dissolve the

covenant into which the sons of God, by his grace, are taken. " If his children forsake my law, and walk not in my judgments ; if they break my statutes, and keep not my commandments ; then will I visit their transgressions with the rod, and their iniquity with stripes. Nevertheless my loving-kindness will I not utterly take from him, nor suffer my faithfulness to fail," Psa. lxxxix. 30—33.

Now, if sin doth not dissolve the covenant, if sin doth not cast me out of this covenant, which is made personally with the Son of God, and into the hands of which, by the grace of God, I am put, then ought I not, though I have sinned, to fear with my first fears.

But again; Sin, after the Spirit of adoption is come, cannot dissolve the relation of father and son, of father and child. And this the church did rightly assert, and that when her heart was under great hardness, and when she had the guilt of erring from his ways ; " Doubtless thou art our Father, though Abraham be ignorant of us, and Israel acknowledge us not," Isa. lxiii. 16.

That sin dissolveth not the relation of father and son is further evident ; " When the fulness of the time was come, God sent forth his Son, made of a woman, made under the law, to redeem them that were under the law, that we might receive the adop- tion of sons. And because ye are sons, God hath sent forth the Spirit of his Son into your hearts, crying, Abba, Father," Gal. iv. 4—6. Now mark, wherefore thou art no more a servant, that is, no more under the law of death and damnation, but a son, and if a son, then an heir of God through Christ, Rom. viii. 17.

Suppose a child doth grievously transgress against

and offend his father, is the relation between them
therefore dissolved? Again; suppose the father
should scourge and chasten the son for such offence,
is the relation between them therefore dissolved?
Yea, suppose the child should now, through ignorance, cry, and say, This man is now no more my
father; is he therefore now no more his father? doth
not every one see the folly of arguings? Why, of the
same nature is that doctrine, that after we have received the Spirit of adoption, the Spirit of bondage
is sent to us again to put us in fear of eternal
damnation.

Know, then, that thy sin, after thou hast received
the Spirit of adoption to cry unto God, Father,
Father, is counted the trangression of a child, not of
a slave, and that all that happeneth to thee for that
transgression, is but the chastisement of a father.
" What son is he whom the father chasteneth not?"
Heb. xii. 7.

It is worth your observation, that the Holy Ghost
checks those who, under their chastisements for sin,
forget to call God their Father. " Ye have," saith
Paul, " forgotten the exhortation which speaketh unto
you as unto children, My son, despise not thou the
chastening of the Lord, nor faint when thou art
rebuked of him," Heb. xii. 5. Yea, observe yet
further, that God's chastising of his children for their
sin, is a sign of grace and love, and not of his wrath,
and thy damnation; therefore now there is no
ground for the aforesaid fear : " For whom the
Lord loveth he chasteneth, and scourgeth every son
whom he receiveth," ver. 6.

Now, if God would not have those that have received the Spirit of the Son, however he chastises
them, to forget the relation that, by the adoption of

sons, they stand in to God, if he checks those that
do forget it, when his rod is upon their backs for
sin ; then it is evident that those fears that thou
hast under a colour of the coming again of the Spirit,
as a Spirit of bondage, to put thee in fear of eternal
damnation, is nothing else but Satan disguised, the
better to play his pranks upon thee.

I will yet give you two or three instances more,
wherein it will be manifest, that whatever happeneth
to thee, I mean as a chastisement for sin, after the
Spirit of adoption is come, thou oughtest to hold fast
by faith the relation of father and son.

The people spoken of by Moses, are said to
have lightly esteemed the Rock of their salvation,
Deut. xxxii. 5, which Rock is Jesus Christ, 1 Cor.
x. 4 ; and that is a grievous sin indeed ; yet, saith
he, " Is not he thy Father that hath bought thee ?"
Deut. xxxii. 6 ; and then puts them upon considering
the days of old.

Those in the prophet Jeremiah had played the
harlot with many lovers, and done evil things as they
could ; and, as another Scripture hath it, gone a
whoring from under their God, yet God calls to them,
by the prophet, saying, " Wilt thou not from this time
cry unto me, My Father, thou art the guide of my
youth ?" Jer. iii. 4.

Remember also that eminent text before mentioned, in 1 Sam. xii. 20 ; " Fear not : ye have done
all this wickedness ;" and labour to maintain faith
in thy soul, of thy being a child, it being true that
thou hast received the Spirit of adoption before, and
so that thou oughtest not to fall under thy first
fears, because the ground is taken away of thy
eternal damnation.

Now, let not any, from what hath been said, take

courage to live loose lives, under a supposition that once in Christ, and ever in Christ, and the covenant cannot be broken, nor the relation of father and child dissolved; for those that do so, it is evident, have not known what it is to receive the Spirit of adoption: it is the spirit of the devil in his own hue that suggesteth this unto them, and that prevaileth with them to do so. Shall we do evil, that good may come? shall we sin, that grace may abound? or shall we be base in life, because God by grace hath secured us from wrath to come? God forbid: these conclusions betoken one void of the fear of God indeed, and of the Spirit of adoption too. For what son is he, that because the father cannot break the relation that is betwixt the father and him, nor suffer sin to do it, that will therefore say, I will live altogether after my own lusts, I will labour to be a continual grief to my father?

Yet, lest the devil, (for some are not ignorant of his devices,) should get an advantage against some of the sons, to draw them away from the filial fear of their Father, let me here, to prevent such temptations, present such with these following considerations.

Though God cannot, and will not, dissolve the relation which the Spirit of adoption hath made betwixt the Father and the sons, for any sin that such do commit: yet he can, and often doth, take away from them the comfort of their adoption, not suffering children, while sinning, to have the sweet and comfortable sense thereof on their hearts. He can allow them to be in the state of the unhappy man to whom it is said, "Snares are round about thee, and sudden fear troubleth thee. Or darkness, that thou canst not see; and abundance of waters cover thee," Job xxii. 10, 11.

God can tell how to hide his face from them, and so to afflict them with that dispensation, that it shall not be in the power of all the world to comfort them. "When he hideth his face, who then can behold him?" Job xxxiv. 29.

God can tell how to make thee again to possess the sins that he long since hath pardoned, and that in such wise that things shall be bitter to thy soul. "Thou writest bitter things against me," saith Job; "and makest me to possess the iniquities of my youth," Job xiii. 26. By this also he once made David groan, and pray against it as an unsupportable affliction, Psa. xxv. 7.

God can lay thee in the dungeon in chains, and roll a stone upon thee; he can make thy feet fast in the stocks, and make thee a gazing stock to men and angels, Lam. iii. 55 ; Job xiii. 27.

God can tell how to cause to cease the sweet operations and blessed influences of his grace in thy soul, and to make those gospel showers that formerly thou hast enjoyed, to become now to thee nothing but powder and dust. See Deut. xxviii. 24.

God can tell how to fight against thee with the sword of his mouth, and to make thee a butt for his arrows; and this is a dispensation most dreadful, Rev. ii. 16 ; Job vi. 4 ; Psa. xxxviii. 2—5.

God can tell how so to bow thee down with guilt and distress, that thou shalt in no wise be able to lift up thy head, Psa. xl. 12.

God can tell how to break thy bones, and to make thee, by reason of that, to live in continual anguish of spirit : yea, he can send a fire into thy bones that

shall burn, and none shall quench it, Psa. li. 8;
Lam. iii. 4; i. 13; Psa. cii. 3; Job xxx. 30.

God can tell how to lay thee aside, and make no
use of thee as to any work for him in thy generation. He can throw thee aside as a broken vessel,
Psa. xxxi. 12; Ezek. xliv. 10—13.

God can tell how to kill thee, and to take thee
away from the earth for thy sins, 1 Cor. xi. 32.

God can tell how to plague thee in thy death,
with great plagues, and of long continuance, Psa.
lxxiii. 4, 5.

What shall I say? God can tell how to let Satan
loose upon thee; when thou liest a dying, he can
license him then to assault thee with great temptations; he can tell how to make thee possess the guilt
of all thy unkindness towards him, and that when
thou, as I said, art going out of the world; he can
cause that thy life shall be in continual doubt before
thee, and not suffer thee to take any comfort day or
night; yea, he can drive thee even to madness with
his chastisements for thy folly, and yet all shall be
done by him to thee as a father chastiseth his son,
Deut. xxviii. 65—67.

Further; God can tell how to tumble thee from off
thy death-bed in a cloud; he can let thee die in the
dark: when thou art dying, thou shalt not know
whither thou art going, to wit, whether to heaven or
to hell. Yea, he can tell how to let thee seem to
come short of life, both in thine own eyes and also
in the eyes of those that behold thee. "Let us
therefore fear," said the apostle, though not with
slavish, yet with filial fear, "lest, a promise being
left us of entering into his rest, any of you should
seem to come short of it," Heb. iv. 1.

Now, all this, and much more, can God do to his,

as a Father by his rod, and Father by rebukes. Ah! who knows, but those that are under them, what terrors, fears, distresses and amazements, God can bring his people into? He can put them into a furnace, a fire, and no tongue can tell what; so unsearchable and fearful are his fatherly chastisements, and yet never give them the Spirit of bondage again to fear. Therefore, if thou art a son, take heed of sin, lest all these things overtake thee, and come upon thee.

Object. But I have sinned, and am under this high and mighty hand of God.

Ans. Then thou knowest what I say is true; but yet take heed of hearkening unto such temptations as would make thee believe thou art out of Christ, under the law, and in a state of damnation: and take heed also, that thou dost not conclude, that the author of these fears is the Spirit of God, come to thee again as a Spirit of bondage, to put thee into such fears, lest unawares to thyself, thou dost deify the devil, dishonour thy Father, overthrow good doctrine, and bring thyself into a double temptation.

Object. But if God deals thus with a man, how can he otherwise think but that he is a reprobate, a graceless, Christless, and faithless one?

Ans. Nay, but why dost thou tempt the Lord thy God? why dost thou sin, and provoke the eyes of his glory? "Wherefore doth a living man complain, a man for the punishment of his sins?" Lam. iii. 39. He doth not willingly afflict, nor grieve the children of men; but if thou sinnest, though God should save thy soul, as he will if thou art an adopted son of God, yet, he will make thee know that sin is sin; and his rod, that he will chastise thee with, if need be, shall be made of scorpions. **Read** the whole book of the Lamentations; read the complaints of Job and David : yea, read what happened to his Son, his wellbeloved, and that when he did but stand in the room of sinners, being in himself altogether innocent, and then consider, O thou sinning child of God, if it is any injustice in God, yea, if it be not necessary, that thou shouldst be chastised for thy sin.

But then, I say, when the hand of God is upon thee, how grievous soever it be, take heed, and beware that thou give not way to thy first fears, lest, as I said before, thou addest to thine affliction. To help thee here, let me give thee a few instances of the conduct of some of the saints under some of the most heavy afflictions that they have met with for sin.

Job was in great affliction, and that, as he confessed, for sin. "I have sinned; what shall I do unto thee, O thou preserver of men? Why hast thou set me as a mark against thee, so that I am a burden to myself?" Job vii. 20; yet he counted not all this as a sign of a damnable state, but as a trial and chastisement; and said, when he was in the hottest of this battle, "When he hath tried me, I shall come forth as gold," Job xxiii. 10. And, again, when he was pressed upon by the tempter to think that God would kill him, he answers with the greatest confidence, "Though he slay me, yet will I trust in him," Job xiii. 15.

David complained that God had broken his bones, that he had set his face against his sins, and had taken from him the joy of his salvation; yet even at this time he saith, "O God, thou God of my salvation," Psa. li. 14.

Heman complained that his soul was full of

troubles, that God had laid him in the lowest pit, that he had put his acquaintance far from him, and was casting off his soul, had hid his face from him, and that he was afflicted from his youth up, and ready to die with trouble. He saith, moreover, that the fierce wrath of God went over him, that his terrors had cut him off; yea, that by reason of them he was distracted, and yet, even before he maketh any of these complaints, he takes fast hold of God as his, saying, "O Lord God of my salvation," Psa. lxxxviii.

The church, in the Lamentations, complains that the Lord had afflicted her for her transgressions, and that in the day of his fierce anger; also, that he had trodden under foot her mighty men, and that he had called the heathen against her: she says, that he had covered her with a cloud in his anger, that he was an enemy, and that he had hung a chain upon her; she adds, moreover, that he had shut out her prayer, broken her teeth with gravel stones, and covered her with ashes; and, in conclusion, that he had utterly rejected her. But what doth she do under all this trial? doth she give up her faith and hope, and return to that fear that begot the first bondage? No; "The Lord is my portion, saith my soul; therefore will I hope in him;" yea, she adds, "O Lord, thou hast pleaded the causes of my soul; thou hast redeemed my life," Lam. iii. 24, 58.

These things show, that God's people, even after they have received the Spirit of adoption, fell foully into sin, and have been bitterly chastised for it; and also, that when the rod was most smart upon them, they made great conscience of not giving way to their first fears wherewith they were made afraid by the Spirit, as it wrought as a Spirit of bondage; for,

indeed, there is no such thing as the coming of the
Spirit of bondage to put us in fear the second time,
as such, that is, after he is come as the Spirit of adoption to the soul.

I conclude, then, that the fear that is wrought by
the Spirit of bondage is good and godly, because the
ground for it is sound ; and I also conclude, that he
comes to the soul as a Spirit of bondage but once,
and that once is before he comes as a Spirit of adoption ; and if, therefore, the same fear doth again
take hold of thy heart, that is, if after thou hast received the Spirit of adoption, thou fearest again the
damnation of thy soul, that thou art out of Christ,
and under the law, that fear is bad, and of the devil,
and ought by no means to be admitted by thee.

Quest. But since it is as you say, how doth the
devil, after the Spirit of adoption is come, work the
child of God into those fears of being out of Christ,
not forgiven, and so an heir of damnation again?

Ans. 1. By giving the lie, and by prevailing
with us to give it too, to the work of grace wrought
in our hearts, and to the testimony of the Holy Spirit
of adoption. Or,

2. By abusing of our ignorance of the everlasting
love of God to his in Christ, and the duration of the
covenant of grace. Or,

3. By abusing some scripture that seems to look
that way, but doth not. Or,

4. By abusing our senses and reason. Or,

5. By strengthening of our unbelief. Or,

6. By overshadowing of our judgment with horrid darkness. Or,

7. By giving us counterfeit representations of
God. Or,

8. By stirring up, and setting in a rage our inward corruptions. Or,

G

9. By pouring into our hearts abundance of horrid blasphemies. Or,

10. By putting wrong constructions on the rod, and chastising hand of God. Or,

1Í. By charging upon us, that our ill behaviour under the rod, and chastising hand of God, is a sign that we indeed have no grace, but are downright graceless reprobates.

By these things, and others like these, Satan bringeth the child of God not only to the borders, but even into the bowels of the fears of damnation, after he hath received a blessed testimony of eternal life, and that by the holy Spirit of adoption.

Quest. But would you not have the people of God stand in fear of his rod, and be afraid of his judgments?

Ans. Yes; and the more they are rightly afraid of them, the less they will come under them, for it is want of fear that brings us into sin, and it is sin that brings us into these afflictions. But I would not have them fear with the fear of slaves, for that will add no strength against sin; but I would have them fear with the reverential fear of sons, and that is the way to depart from evil.

Quest. How is that?

Ans. Why, having before received the Spirit of adoption, still to believe that he is our Father, and so to fear with the fear of children, and not as slaves fear a tyrant. I would, therefore, have them to look upon his rod, rebukes, chidings, and chastisements, and also upon the wrath wherewith he doth inflict, to be but the dispensations of their Father.

This believed, maintains, or at least helps to maintain, in the heart a son-like bowing under the rod.

It also maintains in the soul a son-like confession

of sin, and a justifying of God under all the rebukes
that he grieveth us with. It also engageth us to
come to him, to claim and lay hold of former mercies, to expect more, and to hope a good end shall
be made of all God's present dispensations towards us.

Now, God would have us thus fear his rod, because he is resolved to chastise us therewith, if so
be we sin against him, as I have already shown;
for although God's bowels turn within him, even
while he is threatening his people, yet if we sin, he
will lay on the rod so hard, as to make us cry, "Woe
unto us, that we have sinned!" Lam. v. 16; and,
therefore, as I said, we should be afraid of his judgments, yet only as afore is provided, as of the rod,
wrath, and judgment of a Father.

Quest. But have we any other considerations to
move us to fear God with childlike fear?

I will, in this place, give you five.

Ans. 1. Consider, that God thinks meet to have it
so; and he is wiser in heart than thou; he knows
best how to secure his people from sin, and to that
end hath given them a law and commandments to
read, that they may learn to fear him as a Father.

Ans. 2. Consider, he is mighty in power; if he
touch but with a fatherly touch, man nor angel
cannot bear it; yea, Christ makes use of that argument, he hath power to cast into hell; "Yea, I say
unto you, Fear him," Luke xii. 5.

Ans. 3. Consider, that he is everywhere; thou
canst not be out of his sight or presence, nor out of
the reach of his hand. "Fear ye not me? saith the
Lord," Jer. v. 22. "Can any hide himself in secret
places that I shall not see him? saith the Lord. Do
not I fill heaven and earth? saith the Lord," Jer.
xxiii. 24.

G 2

Ans. 4. Consider, that he is holy, and cannot look with liking upon the sins of his own people.   Therefore, said Peter, "as obedient children, not fashioning yourselves according to the former lusts in your ignorance : but as he which hath called you is holy, so be ye holy in all manner of conversation ; because it is written, Be ye holy ; for I am holy. And if ye call on the Father, who without respect of persons judgeth according to every man's work, pass the time of your sojourning here in fear," 1 Pet. i. 14—17.

Ans. 5. Consider, that he is good, and has been good to thee, good in that he hath singled thee out from others, and saved thee from their death and hell, though thou perhaps was worse in thy life than those that he left when he laid hold on thee.   Oh, how this should engage thy heart to fear the Lord all the days of thy life !   They "shall fear the Lord and his goodness in the latter days," Hos. iii. 5.

And now, for the present, I have done with that fear, I mean as to its first workings, namely, to put us in fear of damnation.

CHAPTER III.

I now come, in the next place, to treat of the grace of fear more immediately intended in the text, which I call a lasting godly fear. And first, by way of explication, by which I shall show,

I. How by the Scripture it is described.

II. I shall show you what this fear flows from.

I. For the first of these,—How by the Scripture this fear is described ; and that,

1. More generally.

2. More particularly.

1. More generally. It is called a grace, that is, a sweet and blessed work of the Spirit of grace, as he is given to the elect. Hence the apostle says, "Let us have grace, whereby we may serve God acceptably with reverence and godly fear," Heb. xii. 28 ; for as that fear that brings bondage is wrought in the soul by the Spirit, as a Spirit of bondage ; so this fear, which is a fear that we have while we are in the liberty of sons, is wrought by him as he manifesteth to us our liberty. "Where the Spirit of the Lord is, there is liberty," 2 Cor. iii. 17 ; that is, where he is a Spirit of adoption, setting the soul free from that bondage under which it was held by the same Spirit, while he

G 3

wrought as a Spirit of bondage.   Hence, as he is
called a Spirit working bondage to fear, so he, as the
Spirit of the Son, and of adoption, is called " The
Spirit of knowledge and of the fear of the Lord,"
Isa. xi. 2.   Because it is that Spirit of grace that is
the author, animator, and maintainer of our filial
fear, or of that fear that is son-like, and that sub-
jecteth the elect unto God, his word, and ways ; unto
him, his word, and ways, as a Father.

This fear is called also " the fear of God," not as
that which is ungodly is, nor yet as that may be,
which is wrought by the Spirit as a Spirit of bondage ;
but by way of eminency, namely, as a dispensation
of the grace of the gospel, and as a fruit of eternal
love.   " I will put my fear in their hearts, that they
shall not depart from me," Jer. xxxii. 40.

This fear of God is called " God's treasure," for it
is one of his choice jewels, it is one of the rarities of
heaven ; " The fear of the Lord is his treasure," Isa.
xxxiii. 6.   And it may well go under such a title, for
as treasure, so the fear of the Lord, is not found in
every corner.   It is said, " All men have not faith,"
2 Thess. iii. 2 ; because that also is more precious than
gold, the same is said about this fear.   " There is
no fear of God before their eyes," Rom. iii. 18 ; that
is, the greatest part of men are utterly destitute of
this goodly jewel, this treasure, the fear of the Lord.
Poor vagrants, when they come straggling to a
lord's house, may perhaps obtain some scraps and
fragments, they may also obtain old shoes, and some
sorry cast-off rags, but they get not any of his jewels ;
they may not touch his choicest treasure; that is
kept for the children, and those that shall be his
heirs.   We may say the same also of this blessed
grace of fear, which is here called God's treasure.

It is only bestowed upon the elect, the heirs and children of the promise; all others are destitute of it, and so continue to death and judgment.

This grace of fear is that which makes men excel, and go beyond all men in the account of God; it is that which beautifies a man, and prefers him above all other. "Hast thou," said God to Satan, "considered my servant Job, that there is none like him in the earth, a perfect and an upright man, one that feareth God, and escheweth evil?" Job i. 8.

Mind it, there is none like him, none like him in the earth. I suppose it is meant either in those parts, or else he was the man that abounded in the fear of the Lord; none like him to fear the Lord: he excelled others with respect to his reverencing of God, bowing before him, and sincerely complying with his will, and therefore is counted the excellent man. It is not the knowledge of the will of God, but our sincerely complying therewith, that proveth we fear the Lord; and it is our so doing that putteth upon us the note of excelling; hereby appears our perfection, herein is manifest our uprightness. A perfect and an upright man is one that feareth God, and that because he escheweth evil.

Therefore this grace of fear is that without which no part or piece of service which we do to God, can be accepted of him. It is, as I may call it, "the salt of the covenant," Lev. ii. 13, which seasoneth the heart, and therefore must not be lacking there; it is also that which salteth or seasoneth all our doings, and therefore must not be lacking in any of them.

I take this grace of fear, to be that which softeneth the heart, and that makes it stand in awe both of the mercies and judgments of God. This is that which

retaineth in the heart that due dread and reverence
of the heavenly Majesty that is meet should both be
in, and kept in the heart of poor sinners. Wherefore when David described this fear, in the exercise
of it, he calls it an awe of God. "Stand in awe,
and sin not," Psa. iv. 4; and again, "My heart
standeth in awe of thy word," Psa. cxix. 161; and
again, "Let all the earth fear the Lord: let all the
inhabitants of the world stand in awe of him," Psa.
xxxiii. 8.

This is that, therefore, that is, as I said before, so
excellent a thing in the eyes of God, namely, a grace
of the Spirit, the fear of God, his treasure, the salt of
the covenant, that which makes men excel all others:
for it is that which makes the sinner to stand in
awe of God, which posture is the most comely thing
in us, throughout all ages. But,

2. More particularly, This grace is called, the
"beginning of knowledge," Prov. i. 7, because by
the first gracious discovery of God to the soul, this
grace is begot; and again, because the first
time that the soul doth apprehend God in Christ
to be good unto it, this grace is animated, by which
the soul is put into a holy awe of God, which
causeth it with reverence and due attention to
hearken to him, and tremble before him. It is also
by virtue of this fear that the soul doth inquire yet
more after the blessed knowledge of God. This is
the more evident, because, where this fear of God is
wanting, or where the discovery of God is not attended with it, the heart still abides rebellious, ob-
stinate, and unwilling to know more, that it might
comply therewith; nay, for want of it, such sinners
say unto God, "Depart from us; for we desire not
the knowledge of thy ways," Job xxi. 14.

This fear is called, "the beginning of wisdom," Psa. cxi. 10, because then, and not till then, a man begins to be truly spiritually wise: what wisdom is there where the fear of God is not? Therefore, the fools are described thus: "For that they hated knowledge, and did not choose the fear of the Lord," Prov. i. 29. The word of God is the fountain of knowledge, into which a man will not with godly reverence look, until he is endued with the fear of the Lord; therefore it is rightly called "the beginning of wisdom: but fools despise wisdom and instruction," Prov. i. 7. It is, therefore, this fear of the Lord that makes a man wise for his soul, for life, and for another world. It is this that teacheth him, how he should escape those spiritual and eternal ruins that the fool is overtaken with, and swallowed up of for ever. A man void of this fear of God, whereever he is wise, or in whatever he excels, yet about the matters of his soul there is none more foolish than himself; for through the want of the fear of the Lord, he leaves the best things at sixes and sevens, and only pursueth with all his heart those that will leave him in the snare when he dies.

This fear of the Lord is to hate evil; to hate sin and vanity. Sin and vanity are the sweet morsels of the fool, and such which the carnal appetite of the flesh runs after; and it is only the virtue that is in the fear of the Lord, that makes the sinner have an antipathy against it. "By the fear of the Lord men depart from evil," Prov. xvi. 6. That is, men shun, separate themselves from, and eschew it in its appearances. Wherefore it is plain, that those that love evil, are not possessed with the fear of God.

There is a generation that will pursue evil, that will take it in, nourish it, lay it up in their hearts, hide it, and plead for it, and rejoice to do it; these cannot have in them the fear of the Lord, for that is to hate it, and to make men depart from it. Where the fear of God and sin are, it will be with the soul as it was with Israel, when Amri and Tibni strove to reign among them both at once; one of them must be put to death; they cannot live together: sin must down, for the fear of the Lord begetteth in the soul a hatred against it, an abhorrence of it; therefore sin must die, that is, as to the affections and lusts of it; for, as Solomon says in another case, "Where no wood is, there the fire goeth out," Prov. xxvi. 20. So we may say, where there is a hatred of sin, and where men depart from it, there it loseth much of its power, waxeth feeble and decayeth. Therefore, Solomon saith again, " Fear the Lord, and depart from evil," Prov. iii. 7; as if he had said, Fear the Lord, and it will follow, that you shall depart from evil: departing from evil, is a natural consequence, a proper effect of the fear of the Lord.

" By the fear of the Lord men depart from evil;" that is, in their judgment, will, mind, and affections; not, that by the fear of the Lord, sin is annihilated, or has lost its being in the soul; there still will be those Canaanites, but they are hated, loathed, abominated, fought against, prayed against, watched against, strove against, and mortified in the soul.

This fear is called a fountain of life. "The fear of the Lord is a fountain of life, to depart from the snares of death," Prov. xiv. 27.

It is a fountain, or spring, which so continually supplies the soul with variety of considerations of sin, of God, of death, and life eternal, as to keep the soul in continual exercise of virtue, and in holy contemplation. It is a fountain of life; every operation thereof, every act and exercise thereof, hath a true and natural tendency to spiritual and eternal felicity. Wherefore the wise man saith, in another place, " The fear of the Lord tendeth to life ; and he that hath it shall abide satisfied; he shall not be visited with evil," Prov. xix. 23. It tendeth to life even as of nature ; everything hath a tendency to that which is most natural to itself, the fire to burn, the water to wet, the stone to fall, the sun to shine, and sin to defile. Thus I say, the fear of the Lord tendeth to life ; the nature of it is to put the soul upon fearing of God, of closing with Christ, and of walking humbly before him.

It is " a fountain of life, to depart from the snares of death." What are the snares of death but sin, the wiles of the devil, etc. From which the fear of God hath a natural tendency to deliver thee, and to keep thee in the way that tendeth to life.

This fear of the Lord is called " the instruction of wisdom," Prov. xv. 33. You heard before that it is the beginning of wisdom; but here you find it called the instruction of wisdom : for indeed it is not only that which makes a man begin to be wise, but to improve, and make advantage of all those helps and means to life, which God hath afforded to that end ; that is, both to his own, and his neighbours' salvation also. It is the instruction of wisdom ; it will make a man capable to use all his natural parts, all his natural wisdom to God's glory, and his own good. There lieth, even in many natural things, that, into which if we were instructed, would yield us a great deal of help to the understanding of spiritual matters ; for in wisdom has God made all the world ; nor is there anything that God has made, whether in heaven above, or on earth beneath, but

there is couched some spiritual mystery in it.   The
which men think of no more than they do the
ground they tread on, or than the stones that are
under their feet, and all because they have not this
fear of the Lord, for had they that, it would teach
them to think, even from that knowledge of God, that
hath by the fear of him been put into their hearts, that
he being so great and so good, there must needs be
abundance of wisdom in the things he hath made :
that fear would also endeavour to find out what that
wisdom is, yea, and give to the soul the instruction
of it.

In that it is called the instruction of wisdom, it
intimates to us, that its tendency is to keep all even,
and in good order in the soul.   When Job perceived
that his friends did not deal with him in an even
spirit and orderly manner, he said that they forsook the fear of the Almighty, Job vi. 14.   For, this
fear keeps a man, even in his words and judgment
of things.   It may be compared to the ballast of the
ship, and to the poise of the balance of the scales, it
keeps all even, and also makes us steer our course
right with respect to the things that pertain to God
and man.

II. I come now to the next thing, namely, to show
you what this fear of God flows from.

This fear, this grace of fear, this son-like fear of
God, flows from the distinguishing love of God to his
elect.   "I will be their God," saith he, "and I will
put my fear in their hearts."   None other obtain it
but those that are inclosed and bound up in that
bundle.   Therefore, in the same place, they are said
to be those that are wrapped up in the eternal or everlasting covenant of God, and so designed to be the
people that should be blessed with this fear.   "I will

make an everlasting covenant with them," saith
God, "that I will not turn away from them, to do
them good; but I will put my fear in their hearts,
that they shall not depart from me," Jer. xxxii. 40.
This covenant declares unto men that God hath,
in his heart, distinguishing love for some of the
children of men; for he saith he will be their God,
that he will not leave them, nor yet suffer them to
depart finally from him. Into these men's hearts
he doth put his fear, this blessed grace, and this rare
and effectual sign of his love, and of their eternal
salvation.

This fear flows from a new heart. This fear is
not in men by nature: the fear of devils they may
have, as also an ungodly fear of God; but this fear
is nót in any, but where there dwelleth a new heart,
which is another fruit and effect of this everlasting
covenant, and of this distinguishing love of God. "A
new heart also will I give you," Ezek. xxxvi. 26.
A new heart, what is that? why, the prophet Jeremiah saith, in another place, "A heart to fear me,"
Jer. xxxii. 39, a circumcised one, a sanctified one.

So then, until a man receive a heart from God,
a heart from heaven, a new heart, he has not this
fear of God in him. Men do not " put new wine into
old bottles: else the bottles break, and the wine
runneth out, and the bottles perish: but they put
new wine into new bottles, and both are preserved,"
Matt. ix. 17.

This fear of God must not be, cannot be found in
old hearts: old hearts are not bottles out of which
this fear of God proceeds; but it is from a honest and
good heart, from a new one, from such an one that
is also an effect of the everlasting covenant, and love
of God to men.

H

"I will give them a heart to fear me;" there must in all actions be heart, and without heart no action is good; nor can there be faith, love, or fear, from every kind of heart; these must flow from such an one, whose nature is to produce and bring forth such fruit; "For of thorns men do not gather figs, nor of a bramble bush gather they grapes," Luke vi. 44; so from a corrupt heart there cannot proceed such fruit as the fear of God, as to believe in God, and love God.

The heart naturally is "deceitful above all things, and desperately wicked," how then should there flow from such a one the fear of God? It cannot be. He therefore that hath not received, at the hands of God, a new heart, cannot fear the Lord.

This fear of God flows from an impression, a sound impression that the word of God maketh on our souls; for without an impress of the word, there is no fear of God. Hence it is said, that God gave to Israel good laws, statutes, and judgments, that they might learn them, and in learning them, learn to fear the Lord -their God, Deut. iv. 8. Therefore saith God, in another place, "Gather the people together, men, and women, and children, and thy stranger that is within thy gates, that they may hear, and that they may learn, and fear the Lord your God," Deut. xxxi. 12.

For as a man drinketh good doctrine into his soul, so he feareth God. . If he drinks it in much, he feareth him greatly; if he drinks it in but little, he feareth him but little; if he drinks it not in at all, he feareth him not at all.

This, therefore, teacheth us how to judge who feareth the Lord; they are those that learn, and that stand in awe of the word: those fear God that have, by the holy word of God, the very form of itself engraven upon the face of their souls. But, on the contrary, those fear not God that do not love good doctrine, that give not place to the wholesome truths of the God of heaven revealed in his testament, to take place in their souls, but rather despise it, and the true professors of it. For, as I said before, this fear of God flows from a sound impression that the word of God maketh upon the soul; and, therefore, this godly fear floweth from faith, for where the word maketh sound impression on the soul, by that impression is faith begotten, whence also this fear doth flow. Therefore, the right hearing of the word is called "the hearing of faith," Gal. iii. 2. Hence it is said again; "By faith Noah, being warned of God of things not seen as yet, moved with fear, prepared an ark to the saving of his house; by the which he condemned the world, and became heir of the righteousness which is by faith," Heb. xi. 7. The word, the warning that he had from God of things not seen as yet, wrought, through faith therein, that fear of God in his heart, that made him prepare against unseen dangers, and that he might be an inheritor of unseen happiness.

Where, therefore, there is not faith in the word of God, there can be none of this fear : and where the word doth not make sound impression on the soul, there can be none of this faith. So that as vices hang together, and have the links of a chain, dependant one upon another, even so the graces of the Spirit also are the fruits of one another, and have such dependance on each other, that the one cannot be without the other. No faith, no fear of God; devils' faith, devils' fear; saints' faith, saints' fear.

This godly fear also floweth from sound repent-

ance for and from sin; godly sorrow worketh repentance, and godly repentance produceth this fear.
"For behold," says Paul, "this selfsame thing,
that ye sorrowed after a godly sort, what carefulness
it wrought in you, yea, what clearing of yourselves,
yea, what indignation, yea, what fear," 2 Cor. vii. 11.
Repentance is the effect of sorrow, and sorrow is the
effect of smart, and smart the effect of faith: now,
therefore, fear must needs be an effect of, and flow
from repentance.

Sinner, do not deceive thyself; if thou art a
stranger to sound repentance, which standeth in
sorrow and shame before God for sin, as also in
turning from it, thou hast no fear of God; I mean
none of this godly fear, for that is the fruit of, and
floweth from sound repentance.

This godly fear also flows from a sense of the love
and kindness of God to the soul. Where there is no
sense or hope of the kindness and mercy of God by
Jesus Christ, there can be none of this fear, but
rather wrath and despair, which produceth that fear
that is either devilish, or else that which is only
wrought in us by the Spirit as a Spirit of bondage;
wherefore the godly fear that now I treat of, floweth
from some sense or hope of mercy from God by
Jesus Christ. "If thou, Lord," said David,
"shouldest mark iniquities, O Lord, who shall
stand? but there is forgiveness with thee, that thou
mayest be feared," Psa. cxxx. 3, 4.

"There is forgiveness with thee." This the soul
has sense of an hope in, and therefore feareth God.
Indeed, nothing can lay a stronger obligation upon
the heart to fear God, than sense of, or hope in mercy.
This begetteth true tenderness of heart, true godly
softness of spirit; this truly endeareth the affections

to God ; and in this true tenderness, softness, and endearedness of affection to God, lieth the very essence of this fear of the Lord, as is manifest by the fruit of this fear when we shall come to speak of it.

This fear of God flows from a due consideration of the judgments of God, that are to be executed in the world, yea upon professors too : yea, further, God's people themselves, I mean, as to themselves, have such a consideration of his judgments towards them, as to produce this godly fear.

When ,God's judgments are in the earth, they effect the fear of his name in the ' hearts of his own people. " My flesh trembleth for fear of thee," said David ; " and I am afraid of thy judgments," Psa. cxix. 120. When God smote Uzza, " David was afraid of God that day," 1 Chron. xiii. 12. Indeed, many regard not the works of the Lord, nor take notice of the operation of his hands, and such cannot fear the Lord. But others observe and regard, and wisely consider of his doings, and of the judgments that he executeth, and that makes them fear the Lord.

This God himself suggesteth as a means to make us fear him. Hence he commanded the false prophet to be stoned, " that all Israel might hear and fear." Hence also he commanded that the rebellious son should be stoned, " that all Israel might hear and fear." The false witness was also to have the same judgment of God executed upon him, " that all Israel might hear and fear." The man also that did aught presumptuously was to die, " that all Israel might hear and fear," Deut. xiii. 11 ; xxi. 21 ; xvii. 13 ; xix. 20.

There is a natural tendency in judgments, as judgments, to beget a fear of God in the heart of man as

man: but when the observation of the judgments of
God is made by him that hath a principle of true
grace in his soul, that observation being made, I say,
by a gracious heart, produceth a fear of God in the
soul, of its own nature, namely, a gracious or godly
fear of God.

This godly fear also flows from a godly remembrance of our former distresses, when we were distressed with our first fears ; for though our first fears
were begotten in us by the Spirit's working as a
Spirit of bondage, and so are not always to be enter-
tained as such, yet even that fear leaveth in us, and
upon our spirits, that sense and relish of our first
awakenings and dread, as also occasions and pro-
duces this godly fear. "Take heed to thyself,"
said God, "and keep thy soul diligently, lest thou
forget the things which thine eyes have seen, and
lest they depart from thy heart all the days of thy
life: but teach them thy sons, and thy sons' sons,"
Deut. iv. 9. But what were the things that their
eyes had seen, that would so condemn them, should
they be forgotten? The answer is, the things which
they saw at Horeb; namely, the fire, the smoke, the
darkness, the earthquake, and their first awakenings
by the law, by which they were brought into a bondage
fear; yea, they were to remember this especially.
"Specially," saith he, "the day that thou stoodest
before the Lord thy God in Horeb, when the Lord
said unto me, Gather me the people together, and
I will make them hear my words, that they may
learn to fear me all the days that they shall live upon
the earth," ver. 10. The remembrance of what we
saw, felt, feared, and trembled under the sense of,
when our first fears were upon us, is that which will
produce in our hearts this godly filial fear.

This godly fear flows from our receiving an answer of prayer, when we supplicated for mercy at the hand of God. See the proof for this. " If there be in the land famine, if there be pestilence, blasting, mildew, locust, or if there be caterpillar; if their enemy besiege them in the land of their cities; whatsoever plague, whatsoever sickness there be; what prayer and supplication soever be made by any man, or by all thy people Israel, which shall know every man the plague of his own heart, and spread forth his hands toward this house : then hear thou in heaven thy dwelling-place, and forgive, and do, and give to every man according to his ways, whose heart thou knowest; (for thou, even thou only, knowest the hearts of all the children of men;) that they may fear thee all the days that they live in the land which thou gavest unto our fathers," 1 Kings viii. 37—40.

This grace of fear also flows from a blessed con-viction of the all-seeing eye of God ; that is, from a belief that he certainly knoweth the heart, and seeth every one of the turnings and returnings thereof, this is intimated in the text last mentioned. " Whose heart thou knowest; that they may fear thee;" namely, so many of them as be, or shall be convinced of this. Indeed, without this conviction, this godly fear cannot be in us; the want of this conviction made the Pharisees such hypocrites. " Ye are they," said Christ, "which justify yourselves before men ; but God knoweth your hearts," Luke xvi. 15. The Pha-risees were not aware of this, therefore they so much preferred themselves before those that by far were better than themselves ; and it is for want of this con-viction that men go on in such secret sins as they do, so much without fear either of God or his judgments.

This grace of fear also flows from a sense of the

impartial judgment of God upon men according to their works. This also is manifest from the text mentioned before : "And give to every man according to his ways," or works, " that they may fear thee." This is also manifest by that passage of Peter ; " And if ye call on the Father, who without respect of persons judgeth according to every man's work, pass the time of your sojourning here in fear," 1 Pet. i. 17. He that hath godly conviction of this, will fear God, will fear before him ; by which fear their hearts are poised, and works directed with trembling, according to the will of God.

Thus you see what a weighty and great grace this grace of the holy fear of God is, and how all the graces of the Holy Ghost yield mutually their help and strength to the nourishment and life of it ; and also how it flows from them all, and hath a dependance upon every one of them, for its due working in the heart of him that hath it. And thus much to show you from whence it flows.

CHAPTER IV.

THE EFFECTS OF GODLY FEAR.

HAVING showed you what godly fear flows from, I come now to show you what proceeds or flows from this godly fear of God, when it is seated in the heart of man.

1. There flows from this godly fear, a devout reverence of God. David says, " God is greatly to be feared in the assembly of the saints," Psa. lxxxix. 7. God, as I have already showed you, is the proper object of godly fear; it is his person and majesty that this fear always causeth the eye of the soul to be upon. " Behold," said David, " as the eyes of servants look unto the hand of their masters, and as the eyes of a maiden unto the hand of her mistress ; so our eyes wait upon the Lord our God, until that he have mercy upon us," Psa. cxxiii. 2.

Nothing aweth the soul that feareth God so much as doth the glorious majesty of God. His person is above all things feared by them ; " I fear God," said Joseph, Gen. xlii. 18 ; that is, more than any other ; I stand in awe of him ; he is my dread, he is my fear ; I do all my actions as in his presence, as in his sight ; I reverence his holy and glorious majesty, doing all things as with fear and trembling before him.

This fear also makes them have a very great reverence of his word ; for that also, I told you, was the rule of their fear. "Princes," said David, "have persecuted me without a cause : but my heart standeth in awe of thy word," Psa. cxix. 161.

From this grace of fear, therefore, flows reverence of the words of God. Of all laws, that man feareth the word; and no law that is not agreeing therewith.

There flows from this godly fear tenderness of God's glory. This fear, I say, will cause a man to afflict his soul, when he seeth that by professors dishonour is brought to the name of God, and to his word. "Who would not fear thee, O King of nations?" said Jeremiah, "for to thee doth it appertain," Jer. x. 7. He speaks it as being affected with that dishonour, that by the body of the Jews was continually brought to his name, his word, and ways; he also speaks it of a hearty wish that they once would be otherwise minded. The same saying, in effect, hath also John in the Revelation; "Who shall not fear thee, O Lord, and glorify thy name?" Rev. xv. 4; clearly concluding, that godly fear produceth a godly tenderness of God's glory in the world, for that appertaineth unto him : that is, it is due unto him, it is a debt which we owe unto him. "Give unto the Lord," said David, "the glory due unto his name," Psa. xxix. 2. Now, if there be begotten in the heart of the godly, by this grace of fear, a godly tenderness of the glory of God, then it follows, of consequence, that where those that have this fear of God, do see his glory diminished by the wickedness of the children of men, there they are grieved and deeply distressed. "Rivers of waters," said David, "run down mine eyes, because they keep not thy law," Psa. cxix. 136. Let me give you for this these following instances.

How was David provoked when Goliath defied the God of Israel! 1 Sam. xvii. 45, 46. Also, when others reproached God, he tells us that such reproach was even as a sword in his bones, Psa. xlii. 10. David, also, for the love that he had to the glory of God's word, ran the hazard and reproach of all the mighty people, Psa. lxxxix. 50. How was Hezekiah afflicted when Rabshakah railed upon his God! Isa. xxxvii. 3, 4. How tender of the glory of God were Eli, Daniel, and the three children, in their day! Eli died with fear and trembling of heart when he heard that the ark of God was taken, 1 Sam. iv. 18. Daniel ran the danger of the lions' mouths, for the tender love that he had to the word and worship of God, Dan. vi. 10—16. The three children ran the hazard of a burning fiery furnace, rather than they would dare to dishonour the way of their God, Dan. iii. 13—30.

This, therefore, is one of the fruits of this godly fear, namely, a reverence of his name, and tenderness of his glory.

2. There flows from this godly fear, watchfulness: as it is said of Solomon's servants, they watched about his bed because of fear in the night, Sol. Song, iii. 7; so it may be said of those that have this godly fear, it makes them a watchful people.

It makes them watch their hearts, and take heed to keep them with all diligence, lest they should, by one or another of its sleights, lead them to do that which in itself is wicked.

It makes them watch, lest some temptation from hell should enter into their heart to the destroying of them.

It makes them watch their mouths, and keep

them also, sometimes as with a bit and bridle, that they offend not with their tongue, knowing that the tongue is apt, being an evil member, soon to catch the fire of hell, to the defiling of the whole body, James iii. 2—10.

It makes them watch over their ways, look well to their goings, and to make strait paths for their feet, Psa. xxxix. 1 ; Heb. xii. 13.

Thus this godly fear puts the soul upon its watch, lest from the heart within, or from the devil without, or from the world, or some other temptation, something should surprise, and overtake the child of God, to defile him, or to cause him to defile the ways of God, and so offend the saints, open the mouths of men, and cause the enemy to speak reproachfully of religion.

3. There flows from this fear a holy provocation to a reverential converse with saints in their religious and godly assemblies, for their further progress in the faith and way of holiness. "Then they that feared the Lord spake often one to another:" spake, that is of God, and his holy and glorious name, kingdom, and works, for their mutual edification. "And a book of remembrance was written before him for them that feared the Lord, and that thought upon his name," Mal. iii. 16.

The fear of the Lord in the heart, provoketh to this in all its acts, not only of necessity, but of nature; it is the natural effect of this godly fear, to exercise the church in the contemplation of God, together and apart. All fear, good and bad, hath a natural propensity in it to incline the heart to contemplate the object of fear, and though a man should labour to take off his thoughts from the object of his fear; whether that object were men, hell, devils, etc., yet do what he could, the next time his fear had any act in it, it would return again to its object. And so it is with godly fear, it will make a man speak of, and think upon the name of God reverentially. Yea, and exercise himself in the holy thoughts of him in such sort, that his soul shall be sanctified and seasoned with such meditations.

Indeed, holy thoughts of God, such as you see this fear doth exercise the heart withal, prepare the heart to and for God. This fear, therefore, is that David prayed for, for the people, when he said, "O Lord God of Abraham, Isaac, and of Israel, our fathers, keep this for ever in the imagination of the thoughts of the heart of thy people, and prepare their heart unto thee," 1 Chron. xxix. 18.

4. There flows from this fear of God, great reverence of his majesty, in and under the use and enjoyment of God's holy ordinances. His ordinances are his courts and palaces, his walks and places, where he giveth his presence to those that wait upon him in them, in the fear of his name. And this is the meaning of the apostle ; " Then had the churches rest throughout all Judea and Galilee and Samaria, and were edified ; and walking in the fear of the Lord, and in the comfort of the Holy Ghost, were multiplied," Acts ix. 31.

" And walking,"—that word intends their use of the ordinances of God. "Walking in all the commandments and ordinances of the Lord blameless," Luke i. 6 ; this, in Old Testament language, is called treading God's courts, and walking in his paths. This, saith the text, they did here " in the fear of the Lord ;" that is, in a great reverence of that God whose ordinances they were. " Ye shall keep my

I

sabbaths, and reverence my sanctuary : I am the Lord," Levit. xix. 30.

It is one thing to be conversant in God's ordinances, and another to be conversant in them with a due reverence of the majesty and name of that God whose ordinances they are; it is common for men to do the first, but none can do the last without this fear. " In thy fear," said David, " will I worship," Psa. v. 7. It is this fear of God, therefore, from whence doth flow that great reverence that his saints have in them, of his majesty in and under the use and enjoyment of God's holy ordinances ; and consequently, that makes our service in the performance of them acceptable to God through Christ.

For God expects that we serve him with fear and trembling, and it is odious among men for a man, in the presence or about the service of his prince, to behave himself lightly, and without due reverence of that majesty, in whose presence and about whose business he is : and if so, how can their service to God have anything like acceptance from the hand of God, that is done, not in, but without the fear of God! This service must needs be an abomination to him, and these servers must come off with rebuke.

5. There flows from this godly fear of God self-denial ; that is, an holy abstaining from those things that are either unlawful or inexpedient; according to that text of Nehemiah; " The former governors that had been before me were chargeable unto the people, and had taken of them bread and wine, beside forty shekels of silver; yea, even their servants bare rule over the people: but so did not I, because of the fear of God," Neh. v. 15. Here now was

self-denial, he would not do as they did that went
before him, neither himself, nor should his servants;
but what was it that put him upon these acts of self-
denial? The answer is, the fear of God: "But so
did not I, because of the fear of God."

Now, whether by the fear of God, in this place, be
meant his word, or the grace of fear in his heart,
may perhaps be a scruple to some, but in my judgment the text must have respect to the latter, namely,
to the grace of fear, for without that be indeed in the
heart, the word will not produce that good self-denial
in us, of which here you find this good man lived in
the daily exercise.

The fear of God, therefore, was the cause of
his self-denial, was this grace of fear in his heart.
This made him to be, as was said before, tender of
the honour of God, and of the salvation of his
brother: yea, so tender, that rather than he would
give an occasion to the weak to stumble, or be
offended, he would even deny himself of that, which
others never hesitated to do. Paul, also, through the
sanctifying operations of this fear of God in his
heart, did deny himself even of lawful things, for the
profit of his brother. "I will eat no flesh while the
world standeth, lest I make my brother to offend,"
1 Cor. viii. 13; that is, if his eating of it would
make his brother to offend.

Men that have not this fear of God in them, will
not, cannot deny themselves, (of love to God, and
the good of the weak, who are subject to stumble at
indifferent things;) but where this grace of fear is,
there follows self-denial; there men are tender of
offending, and count that it far better becomes their
profession to be of a self-denying, condescending
conversation and temper, than to stand sturdily to

their own liberty in things inexpedient, whoever is offended thereat.

This grace of fear, therefore, is a very excellent thing, because it yieldeth such excellent fruit as this. For this self-denial, of how little esteem soever it be with some, yet the want of it, if the words of Christ be true, as they are, takes quite away, from even a professor, the very name of a disciple, Matt. x. 37, 38; Luke xiv. 27.

They, says Nehemiah, lorded it over the brethren, but so did not I. They took bread and wine, and forty shekels of silver of them, but so did not I: yea, even their servants bare rule over the people, but so did not I, because of the fear of God, Neh. v. 15.

6. There flows from this godly fear of God, " singleness of heart," Col. iii. 22. Singleness of heart both to God and man; singleness of heart, that is it which, in another place, is called sincerity, and godly simplicity; and it is this, when a man doth a thing simply for the sake of him, or of the law, that commands it, without respect to this by-end, or that desire of praise or of vain-glory from others. I say, when our obedience to God is done by us simply, or alone for God's sake, for his word's sake, without any regard to this or that by-end or reserve, "not with eye-service, as men-pleasers; but with singleness of heart fearing God." A man is more subject to nothing than to swerve from singleness of heart in his service to God, and obedience to his will.

How doth the Lord charge the children of Israel, and all their obedience, and that for seventy years together, with the want of singleness of heart towards him! " When ye fasted and mourned in the fifth and seventh month, even those seventy years, did ye at all fast unto me, even to me? And when ye did

eat, and when ye did drink, did not ye eat for yourselves, and drink for yourselves ?" Zech. vii. 5, 6.

They wanted this singleness of heart in their
fasting and in their eating, in their mourning and
in their drinking ; they had double hearts in what
they did. They did not as the apostle bids,
" Whether therefore ye eat, or drink, or whatsoever
ye do, do all to the glory of God," 1 Cor. x. 31.
And the reason of their want of this thing was, they
wanted this fear of God; for that, as the apostle here
saith, effecteth singleness of heart to God, and makes
a man, as John said of Gaius, do faithfully whatever
he doth, 3 John 5. And the reason is, as hath
been already urged, for that grace of fear of God retaineth, and keepeth upon the heart, a reverential and
awful sense of the dread majesty and all-seeing eye
of God; also a due consideration of the day of account
before him : it likewise maketh his service sweet
and pleasing, and fortifies the soul against all dis-
couragements. By this means, I say, the soul in its
service to God or man, is not so soon captivated, as
where there is not this fear ; but through and by it
its service is accepted, being single, sincere, simple,
and faithful; when others, with what they do, are
cast into hell for their hypocrisy, for they mix not
what they do with godly fear.

Singleness of heart in the service of God is of
such absolute necessity, that without it, as I have
hinted, nothing can be accepted, because where that
is wanting, there wanteth love to God, and to that
which is true holiness indeed. It was this singleness of heart that made Nathanael so honourable in
the eyes of Jesus Christ. " Behold," said he, " an
Israelite indeed, in whom is no guile," John i. 47.

And it was the want of it that made him so much abhor the Pharisees. They wanted sincerity, simplicity, and godly sincerity in their souls, and so became an abhorrence in his esteem. Now, I say this golden grace, singleness of heart, flows from this godly fear of God.

7. There flows from this godly fear of God, compassion and bowels to those of the saints that are in necessity and distress. This is manifest in good Obadiah. It is said of him, that he "took an hundred prophets, and hid them by fifty in a cave, and fed them with bread and water," 1 Kings xviii. 4; and this was in the days when Jezebel, that tyrant, sought their lives to destroy them. But what was it that moved so upon his heart as to cause him to do this thing? why, it was this blessed grace of the fear of God. "Now Obadiah," saith the text, "feared the Lord greatly: for it was so, when Jezebel cut off the prophets of the Lord, that Obadiah took an hundred prophets, and hid them by fifty in a cave, and fed them with bread and water." This was charity to the distressed, even to the distressed for the Lord's sake.

Had not Obadiah feared the Lord, yea, had he not greatly feared him, he would not have been able to do this thing, especially as the case then stood with him, and also with the church at that time; for then Jezebel sought to slay all that indeed feared the Lord; yea, and the persecution prevailed so much at that time, that even Elijah himself thought that she had killed all but him. But now, even now, the fear of God in this good man's heart, put forth itself into acts of mercy though attended with so imminent danger.

See here, therefore, that the fear of God will put forth itself in the heart where God hath put it, to show kindness, and to have compassion upon the distressed servants of God, in the very neighbourhood of Jezebel's court; for Obadiah dwelt in Ahab's house, and Jezebel was Ahab's wife, and an horrible persecutor, as was said before : yet Obadiah would show mercy to the poor, because he feared God, yea, he would venture her displeasure, his place, and neck, and all, but he will be merciful to his brethren in distress.

Cornelius, also, being a man possessed with this fear of God, became a very free-hearted and open-handed man to the poor. He feared God, and gave much alms to the people. Indeed this fear, this godly fear of God, is an universal grace; it will stir up the soul unto all good duties. It is a fruitful grace, from it ever floweth abundance of excellent virtues, nor without it can there be any thing good, or done well that is done.

8. There flows from this fear of God, hearty, fervent, and constant prayer. This also is seen in Cornelius, that devout man. He " feared God;" and what then? why, he " gave much alms to the people, and prayed to God alway," Acts x. 2.

Did I say that hearty, fervent, and constant prayer, flowed from this fear of God? I will add, that if the whole duty, and the continuation of it, be not managed with this fear of God, it profiteth nothing at all. It is said of our Lord Jesus Christ himself, " He was heard in that he feared," Heb. v. 7. He prayed, then, because he feared, because he feared God, and therefore was his prayer accepted of him, even because he feared.

This godly fear is so essential to right prayer, and

right prayer is such an inseparable effect and fruit of this fear, that thou must have both or none; he that prayeth not, feareth not God; yet he that prayeth not fervently and frequently, feareth him not; and so he that feareth him not, cannot pray; for if prayer be the effect of this fear of God, then without this fear, prayer, fervent prayer, ceaseth. How can those pray, or make conscience of the duty, that fear not God? O prayerless man, thou fearest not God! Thou wouldest not live so long like a swine or a dog in the world as thou dost, if thou fearedst the Lord.

9. There floweth from this fear of God a readiness and willingness, at God's call, to give up our best enjoyments to his disposal. This is evident in Abraham, who, at God's call, without delay, rose early in the morning to offer up his only and wellbeloved Isaac a burnt offering, in the place where God should appoint him.

It was a rare thing that Abraham did; and had he not had this rare grace, this fear of God, he would not, he could not, have done to God's liking so wonderful a thing. It is true, the Holy Ghost also makes this service of Abraham to be the fruit of his faith; "By faith Abraham, when he was tried, offered up Isaac: and he that had received the promises offered up his only begotten son," Heb. xi. 17. Aye, and without doubt, love unto God, in Abraham, was not wanting in this his service, nor was this grace of fear; nay, in the history where it is recorded, it is chiefly accounted for as the fruit of his godly fear, and that by an angel from heaven. "And the angel of the Lord called unto him out of heaven, and said, Abraham, Abraham: and he said, Here am I. And he said, Lay not thine hand upon the lad, neither do thou any thing unto him: for now I know that thou fearest God, seeing thou hast not withheld thy son, thine only son from me," Gen. xxii. 11, 12.

Now I know it; now thou hast offered up thine only Isaac, thine all, at the bidding of thy God. Now I know it. The fear of God is not presently discerned in the heart and life of a man. Abraham had long before this done many a holy duty, and showed much willingness of heart to observe and do the will of God; yet you find not, as I remember, that he had this testimony from heaven that he feared God till now: but now he has it, now he has it from heaven. "Now I know that thou fearest God." Many duties may be done (though I do not say that Abraham did them) without the fear of God; but when a man shall not stick at, or withhold his darling from God, when called upon by God to offer it up unto him, that declareth, yea, and gives conviction to angels, that now he feareth God.

10. There floweth from this godly fear, humility of mind. This is evident, because, when the apostle cautions the Romans against the venom of spiritual pride, he directs them to the exercise of this blessed grace of fear as its antidote. "Be not highminded," saith he, "but fear," Rom. xi. 20. Pride, spiritual pride, which is here set forth by the word "highminded," is a sin of a very high and damnable nature; it was the sin of the fallen angels, and is that which causeth men to fall into the same condemnation; "Lest being lifted up with pride, he fall into the condemnation of the devil," 1 Tim. iii. 6. Pride, I say, condemns a professor with the damnation of devils, with the damnation of hell, and therefore it is a deadly, deadly sin. Now, against this deadly sin is set the grace of humility, that comely garment,

for so the apostle calls it, saying, "Be clothed with humility," 1 Pet. v. 5. But the question is now, How we should attain to, and live in the exercise of this blessed and comely grace? to which the apostle answers, Fear: be afraid with godly fear; and thence will flow humility. "Be not highminded, but fear;" that is, fear, or be continually afraid and jealous of yourselves, and of your own naughty hearts; also fear lest, at some time or other, the devil, your adversary, should get advantage of you. Fear, lest, by forgetting what you are by nature, you also forget the need that you have of continual pardon, support, and supplies from the Spirit of grace, and so grow proud of your own abilities, or of what you have received of God, and fall into the condemnation of the devil. Fear, and that will make you little in your own eyes, keep you humble, put you upon crying to God for protection, and upon lying at his footstool for mercy; that will also make you have low thoughts of your own parts, your own doings, and cause you to prefer your brother before yourself, and so you will walk in humiliation, and be continually under the teachings of God, and under his conduct in your way. God will teach the humble. "The meek will he guide in judgment: and the meek will he teach his way," Psa. xxv. 9.

From this grace of fear, then, flows this excellent and comely thing humility; yea, it also is maintained by this fear. Fear takes off a man from trusting to himself; it puts a man upon trying of all things; it puts a man upon desiring counsel and help from heaven; it makes a man ready and willing to hear instruction, and makes a man walk lowly, softly, and so securely in the way.

11. There flows from this grace of fear,

hope in the mercy of God. "The Lord taketh pleasure in them that fear him, in those that hope in his mercy," Psa. cxlvii. 11. The latter part of the text is an explanation of the former; as if the psalmist had said, Those are the men that fear the Lord, even those that hope in his mercy; for true fear produceth hope in God's mercy. And it is further manifest thus:—Fear, true fear of God inclineth the heart to a serious inquiry after that way of salvation which God himself hath prescribed; now the way that God hath appointed, by the which the sinner is to obtain the salvation of his soul, is his mercy as set forth in the word; and ·godly fear hath special regard to the word. To this way, therefore, the sinner with this godly fear submits his soul, rolls himself upon it, and so is delivered from that death into which others, for want of this fear of God, do headlong fall.

It is, as I also hinted before, the nature of godly fear to be very much putting the soul upon the inquiry which is, and which is not the thing approved of God, and accordingly to embrace it, or shun it. Now, I say, this fear, having put the soul upon a strict and serious inquiry after the way of salvation, at last it finds it to be by the mercy of God in Christ; therefore this fear putteth the soul upon hoping also in him for eternal life and blessedness; by which hope he doth not only secure his soul, but becomes a person in whom God delights. "The Lord taketh pleasure in them that fear him, in those that hope in his mercy," Psa. cxlvii. 11.

Besides, this godly fear carrieth in it self-evidence that the state of the sinner is happy, because possessed with this happy grace. Therefore, as John saith, "We know that we have passed from death

unto life, because we love the brethren," 1 John
iii. 14. So here, "The Lord taketh pleasure in them
that fear him, in those that hope in his mercy." If
I fear God, and if my fearing of him is a thing in
which he taketh such pleasure, then may I boldly
venture to roll myself for eternal life into the bosom
of his mercy, which is Christ.

This fear also produceth hope; if, therefore, poor
sinner, thou knowest thyself to be one that is possessed with this fear of God, suffer thyself to be per-
suaded therefore to hope in the mercy of God for
salvation, for the Lord takes pleasure in thee; and
it delights him to see thee hope in his mercy.

12. There floweth from this godly fear of
God, an honest and conscientious use of all those
means which God hath ordained that we should be
conversant in for our attaining salvation. Faith and
hope in God's mercy secureth our justification
and hope, and, as you have heard, they flow from
this fear. But now, besides faith and hope, there
is a course of life in those things in which God
hath ordained us to have our conversation, without
which there is no eternal life. "Ye have your fruit
unto holiness, and the end everlasting life," Rom.
vi. 22; and again, "Holiness, without which no man
shall see the Lord," Heb. xii. 14. Not that faith and
hope are deficient, if they be right, but they are
both of them counterfeit when not attended with a
reverent use of all the means: upon the reverent use
of which the soul is put by this grace of fear.
"Wherefore, my beloved," said Paul, "as ye have
always obeyed, not as in my presence only, but now
much more in my absence, work out your own salvation with fear and trembling," Phil. ii. 12.

There is a faith and hope of mercy, that may de-

ceive a man, because they are alone, and not attended
with those companions that accompany salvation;
but now this godly fear carries in itself, not only a
moving of the soul to faith and hope in God's
mercy, but an earnest provocation to the holy and
reverent use of all the means that God has ordained
for a man to have his conversation in, in order to his
eternal salvation.

"Work out your salvation with fear." Not that
work is meritorious, or such that can purchase eternal
life; for eternal life is obtained by hope in God's
mercy; but this hope, if it be right, is attended with
this godly fear, which fear putteth the soul upon a
diligent use of all those means that may tend to the
strengthening of hope, and so to the making of us
holy in all manner of conversation, that we may be
" meet to be partakers of the inheritance of the saints
in light." For hope purifieth the heart, if fear of
God be its companion, and so maketh a man a
vessel of mercy prepared unto glory. Paul bids
Timothy to flee pride, covetousness, doting about
questions, and the like, and to " follow after righteousness, godliness, faith, love, patience, meekness.
Fight the good fight of faith, lay hold of eternal
life," 1 Tim. vi. 11, 12.

So Peter says, "Add to your faith virtue;
and to virtue knowledge; and to knowledge temperance; and to temperance patience; and to patience godliness; and to godliness brotherly kindness; and to brotherly kindness charity. For if these
things be in you, and abound, they make you that ye
shall neither be barren nor unfruitful in the knowledge of our Lord Jesus Christ.—Wherefore the
rather, brethren, give diligence to make your calling
and election sure: for if ye do these things, ye shall

never fall: for so an entrance shall be ministered
unto you abundantly into the everlasting kingdom of
our Lord and Saviour Jesus Christ," 2 Pet. i. 5—11.
The sum of all which is, that which was mentioned before, namely, to work out our own salvation
with fear and trembling. For none of these things
can be conscientiously done but by and with the help
of this blessed grace of fear.

13. There flows from this godly fear a great
delight in the holy commands of God; that is,
a delight to be conformable unto them. "Blessed is
the man that feareth the Lord, that delighteth
greatly in his commandments," Psa. cxii. 1. This
confirmeth that which was said before, namely, that
this fear provoketh to a holy and reverent use of the
means; for that cannot be, when there is not an
holy, yea, a great delight in the commandments.
Wherefore this fear maketh the sinner to abhor that
which is sin, because that is contrary to the object of
his delight. A man cannot delight himself at the
same time in things directly opposite one to another,
as sin, and the holy commandment are; therefore
Christ saith of the servant, he "cannot love God and
mammon;" if he cleaves to the one, he must hate
and despise the other: there cannot, at the same
time, be service to both, because that they are at
enmity one with the other: so are sin and the commandment; therefore, if a man delighteth himself
in the commandment, he hateth that which is opposite, which is sin; how much more when he greatly
delighteth in the commandment!

Now, this holy fear of God taketh the heart and
affections from sin, and setteth them upon the holy
commandment; therefore such a man is rightly esteemed blessed. For no profession makes a man

blessed, but that which is accompanied with an alien-
ation of the heart from sin; nor doth any thing do
that when this holy fear is wanting. It is from this
fear, then, that love to and delight in the holy commandment flow; and so by that the sinner is kept
from those falls and dangers of miscarrying that
other professors are so subject to: he greatly delights
in the commandment.

14. There floweth from this fear of God, en-
largement of heart. "Then thou shalt see, and flow
together, and thine heart shall fear, and be enlarged," Isa. lx. 5. "Thine heart shall fear, and be
enlarged;" enlarged to God-ward, enlarged to his
ways, enlarged to his holy people, enlarged in love
after the salvation of others. Indeed, when this fear
of God is wanting, though the profession be ever so
famous, the heart is shut up, and straitened, and
nothing is done in that princely free spirit, which is
called "the spirit of the fear of the Lord," Isa. xi. 2.
But with grudging, legally, or with desire of vain
glory; this enlargedness of heart is wanting, for that
flows from this fear of the Lord.

Thus have I shown you what this fear of God is,
what it flows from, and also what flows from it.

CHAPTER V.

HAVING thus briefly handled, in particular, thus far this fear of God, I shall now show you certain of the excellent privileges of those that fear the Lord: not that they are not privileges that have been already mentioned; for what greater privilege than to have this fear producing in the soul such excellent things, so necessary for us for good, both with reference to this world and that which is to come; but because those fourteen effects set forth in the preceding chapter, do rather flow from this grace of fear where it is, than from a promise to the person that hath it, therefore I have chosen rather to discourse of them as the fruits and effects of fear than otherwise. Now, besides all these, there are entailed by promise to the man that hath this fear, many other blessed privileges, the which I shall now, in a brief way, lay open unto you.

1. First, then, that man that feareth the Lord has a grant and a licence to trust in the Lord, with an affirmation that the Lord is his help and his shield. "Ye that fear the Lord, trust in the Lord: he is their help and their shield," Psa. cxv. 11. Now, what a privilege is this! An exhortation in general to sinners, as sinners, to trust in him, is a privilege great and glorious; but for a man to be singled out

from his neighbours, for a man to be spoken to from heaven, as it were by name, and to be told that God hath given him a licence, a special and peculiar grant to trust in him, this is abundantly more, and yet this is the grant that God hath given that man. He hath, I say, a licence to do it, a licence indited by the Holy Ghost, and left upon record for those to be born that shall fear the Lord to trust in him. And not only so, but as the text affirms, he is their help and their shield. Their help under all their weaknesses and infirmities, and a shield to defend them against all the assaults of the devil and this world. So then, the man that feareth the Lord is licensed to make the Lord his stay, and the God of his salvation the succour and deliverer of his soul. He will defend him because his fear is in his heart. O ye servants of the Lord, ye that fear him, live in the comfort of this, boldly make use of it when you are in straits, and put your trust under the shadow of his wings, for indeed he would have you do so, because you do fear the Lord.

2. God hath also proclaimed concerning the man that feareth the Lord, that he will also be his teacher and guide in the way that he shall choose; and hath moreover promised concerning such, that their soul shall dwell at ease. "What man is he that feareth the Lord?" said David, "him shall he teach in the way that he shall choose," Psa. xxv. 12.

Now, to be taught of God, what is like it? yea, what like to being taught in the way that thou shalt choose? Thou hast chosen the way to life, God's way, but perhaps thy ignorance about it is so great, and those that tempt thee to turn aside so many, and so subtle, that they seem to outwit thee, and confound thee with their guile. Well, but the Lord whom thou fearest

K 3

will not leave thee to thy ignorance, nor yet to thine enemies power or subtlety, but will take it upon himself to be thy teacher and thy guide, and that in the way that thou hast chosen. Hear then, and behold thy privilege, O thou that fearest the Lord; and whoever wanders, or turns aside, or swerveth from the way of salvation, whoever is benighted and lost in the midst of darkness, thou shalt find the way to the heaven and the glory that thou hast chosen.

Further; He doth not only say that he will teach those the way, for that must of necessity be supplied, but he says also that he will teach such *in* it; " Him shall he teach in the way that he shall choose." This argueth that, as thou shalt know, so the way shall be made, by the communion that thou shalt have with God therein, sweet and pleasant to thee. For this text promiseth unto the man that feareth the Lord, the presence, company, and discovery of the mind of God, while he is going in the way that he hath chosen. It is said of the good scribe, that he is instructed unto, as well as into the way of the kingdom of God, Matt. xiii. 52. " Instructed unto," that is, he hath the heart and mind of God still discovered to him in the way that he hath chosen, even all the way from this world to that which is to come, even until he shall come to the very gate and door of heaven. What the disciples said was the effect of the presence of Christ, namely, that their hearts did burn within them while he talked to them by the way, Luke xxiv. 32, shall be also fulfilled in thee; he will meet with thee in the way, talk with thee in the way, he will teach thee in the way that thou shalt choose.

3. Dost thou fear the Lord? he will open his secret unto thee, even that which he hath hid, and kept close from all the world; namely, the secret

of his covenant, and of thy concern therein. "The secret of the Lord is with them that fear him ; and he will show them his covenant," Psa. xxv. 14. This then further confirms what was said before; his secret shall be with them, and his covenant shall be shown unto them.

His secret, namely, that which hath been kept hid from ages and generations, that which he manifesteth only to the saints, or holy ones ; that is, his Christ, for he it is that is hid in God, and that no man can know but he to whom the Father shall reveal him.

But, oh! what is there wrapped up in this Christ, this secret of God ! why, all the treasures of life, of heaven, and happiness. "In whom are hid all the treasures of wisdom and knowledge," Col. ii. 3 ; yea, "in him dwelleth all the fulness of the Godhead bodily," ver. 9.

He also is that hidden One, who is so full of grace to save sinners, and so full of truth and faithfulness to keep promise and covenant with them, that their eyes must needs convey, even by every glance they make upon his person, offices, and relation, such affecting ravishments to the heart, that it would please those that see him, even to be killed with that sight.

This secret of the Lord shall be ; nay, is with those that fear him, for he dwelleth in their heart by faith. "And he will show them his covenant ;" that is, the covenant that is confirmed of God in Christ, that everlasting and eternal covenant ; and show him too, that he himself is wrapped up therein as in a bundle of life with the Lord his God. These are the thoughts, purposes, and promises of God to those that fear him.

4. Dost thou fear the Lord? His eye is always over thee for good, to keep thee from all evil. "Behold, the eye of the Lord is upon them that fear him, upon them that hope in his mercy; to deliver their soul from death, and to keep them alive in famine," Psa. xxxiii. 18, 19.

His eye is upon them, that is, to watch over them for good. "He that keepeth Israel shall neither slumber nor sleep," Psa. cxxi. 4. His eyes are upon them, and he will keep them as a shepherd doth his sheep; that is, from those wolves that seek to devour them, and to swallow them up in death. His eyes are upon them, for they are the objects of his delight, the rarities of the world, in whom is all his delight. His eye is upon them, as I said before, to teach and instruct them; "I will instruct thee and teach thee in the way which thou shalt go: I will guide thee with mine eye," Psa. xxxii. 8. The eye of the Lord, there-fore, is upon them; not to take advantage of them, to destroy them for their sins, but to guide, to help and deliver them from death, from that death that would feed upon their souls. "To deliver their soul from death, and to keep them alive in famine," Psa. xxx. 19. Take death here for death spiritual and death eternal, and the famine here, not for that which is for want of bread and water, but for that which comes on many for want of the word of the Lord, and then the sense is this:—The man that feareth the Lord, shall neither die spiritually nor eternally, for God will keep him with his eye from all those things that would in such a manner kill him. Again; should there be a famine of the word, should there want both the word and those that preach it in the place where thou dost dwell, yet bread shall be given thee, and thy water shall be sure; thou shalt not die of the famine because thou fearest God. I say that man shall not, behold he shall not, because he fears God; and this the next head doth yet more fully manifest.

5. Dost thou fear God? Fear him for this advantage more and more. "O fear the Lord, ye his saints: for there is no want to them that fear him. The young lions do lack, and suffer hunger: but they that seek the Lord shall not want any good thing," Psa. xxxiv. 9, 10. Not anything that God sees good for them, shall those men want that fear the Lord. If health will do them good; if sickness will do them good; if riches will do them good; if poverty will do them good; if life will do them good; if death will do them good; then they shall not want them: neither shall any of these come nigh them, if they will not do them good.

"The lions," that is, the wicked people of the world, that fear not God, are not made sharers in this great privilege; all things fall out to them contrary, because they fear not God. In the midst of their sufficiency they are in want of that good that God puts into the worst things that the man that feareth God doth meet with in the world.

6. Dost thou fear God? He hath given charge to the armies of heaven to look after, take charge of, to encamp about, and to deliver thee. "The angel of the Lord encampeth round about them that fear him, and delivereth them," Psa. xxxiv. 7. This also is a privilege entailed to them, that in all generations fear the Lord. The angels, the heavenly creatures have it in commission to take the charge of those that fear the Lord; and one of them is able to slay in one night 185,000 men. These are they that encamped about Elisha like horses of

fire and chariots of fire when the enemy came to destroy him. They also helped Hezekiah against the
band of the enemy, because he feared God, 2 Kings
vi. 17; Isa. xxxvii. 36.

The angel of the Lord encampeth round about
them; that is, lest the enemy should set upon them
on any side: but let him come where he will, behind
or before, on this side or that, the angel of the Lord
is there to defend them.

"The angel." It may be spoken in the singular
number, perhaps, to show that every one that feareth
God hath his angel to attend on him and serve him.
When the church, in the Acts, was told that Peter
stood at the door and knocked; at first they counted
the messenger mad, but when she did constantly
affirm it, they said, "It is his angel," Acts xii. 15.
So Christ saith of the children that came unto him,
"Their angels do always behold the face of my
Father which is in heaven," Matt. xviii. 10. "Their
angels;" that is, those of them that feared God, had
each of them his angel, who had a charge from God
to keep them in their way. We little think of this,
yet this is the privilege of those that fear the Lord;
yea, if need be they shall all come down to help
them, and to deliver them, rather than contrary to
the mind of their God they should by any be abused.
"Are they not all ministering spirits, sent forth to
minister for them who shall be heirs of salvation,"
Heb. i. 14.

But how do they deliver them? for so says the
text, "The angel of the Lord encampeth about
them that fear him, and delivereth them."

Ans. The way that they take to deliver those that
fear the Lord, is sometimes by smiting their enemies
with blindness, that they may not find them. And

so they served the enemies of Lot, Gen. xix. 11.
Sometimes by smiting them with deadly fear, and
so they served those that laid siege against Samaria,
2 Kings vii. 6; and sometimes by smiting them
even with death itself, and thus they served Herod,
after he had attempted to kill the apostle James, and
also sought to vex certain others of the church, Acts
xii. 23.   These angels that are servants to those that
fear the Lord, are those that will, if God doth bid
them, revenge the quarrel of his servants upon the
stoutest monarch on earth. This, therefore, is a
glorious privilege of the men that fear the Lord.
Alas, they are some of them so mean, that they are
counted not worth taking notice of by the high ones
of the world, but their betters do respect them, the
angels of God count not themselves too good to
attend on them, and encamp about them to deliver
them.   This, then, is the man that hath his angel to
wait upon him, even he that feareth God.

7. Dost thou fear the Lord?   Salvation is nigh
unto thee.   "Surely his salvation is nigh them that
fear him; that glory may dwell in our land," Psa.
lxxxv. 9.

This is another privilege for those that fear the
Lord. I told you before, that the angel of the Lord
did encamp about them, but now, it is said, his salvation is also nigh them; the which, although it doth
not altogether exclude the conduct of angels, but
include them, yet it looketh further. Surely
his salvation, his saving pardoning grace, is nigh
those that fear him; that is, to save them out of
the hand of their spiritual enemies. The devil,
sin, and death do always wait even to devour
those that fear the Lord, but to deliver them from
these, his salvation doth attend them. So then, if

Satan tempts, here is their salvation nigh; if sin, by breaking forth, beguiles them, here is God's saltion nigh them; yea, if death itself shall suddenly seize upon them, here is their God's salvation nigh them.

8. Dost thou fear the Lord? Hearken yet again; "The mercy of the Lord is from everlasting to everlasting upon them that fear him, and his righteousness unto children's children," Psa. ciii. 17. This still confirms what was last asserted, that is, that his salvation is nigh unto them. His salvation, that is, pardoning mercy, that is nigh them. But mind this, there it is said, it is *nigh* them; but here, it is *upon* them. His mercy is "upon them;" it covereth them all over, it compasseth them about as with a shield. Therefore they are said, in another place, to be clothed with salvation, and covered with the robe of righteousness, Isa. lxi. 10. The mercy of the Lord is upon them, to shelter and defend them. The mercy, the pardoning, preserving mercy, the mercy of the Lord, is upon them, who is he then that can condemn them?

But there yet is more behind; "The mercy of the Lord is from everlasting to everlasting upon them." It was designed for them before the world was, and shall be upon them when the world itself is ended: from everlasting to everlasting it is upon them that fear him. This "from everlasting to everlasting" is that by which, in another place, the eternity of God himself is declared; "From everlasting to everlasting, thou art God," Psa. xc. 2. The meaning then may be this :—That so long as God hath his being, so long shall the man that feareth him find mercy at his hand. According to that word of Moses: "The eternal God is thy refuge, and underneath are the everlasting arms : and he shall thrust out the enemy from before thee; and shall say, Destroy them," Deut. xxxiii. 27.

Child of God, thou that fearest God, here is mercy nigh thee, mercy enough, everlasting mercy upon thee. This is long-lived mercy. It will live longer than thy sin; it will live longer than temptation; it will live longer than thy sorrows; it will live longer than thy persecutors. It is mercy from everlasting, to contrive thy salvation, and mercy to everlasting, to weather it out with all thy adversaries. Now, what can hell and death do to him that hath this mercy of God upon him? And this hath the man that feareth the Lord.

Take that other blessed word, and O thou man that fearest the Lord, hang it like a chain of gold about thy neck. " As the heaven is high above the earth, so great is his mercy toward them that fear him," Psa. ciii. 11. If mercy as big, as high, and as good as heaven itself will be a privilege, the man that feareth God shall have a privilege.

9. Dost thou fear God? " Like as a father pitieth his children, so the Lord pitieth them that fear him," Psa. ciii. 13.

" The Lord pitieth them that fear him ;" that is, condoleth, and is affected; feeleth, and sympathizeth with them in all their afflictions. It is a great matter for a poor man to be in this manner in the affections of the great and mighty, but for a poor sinner to be thus in the heart and affections of God, (and those that fear him are so,) this is astonishing to consider. " In all their affliction he was afflicted, and the angel of his presence saved them : in his love and in his pity he redeemed them; and he bare them, and carried them all the days of old," Isa. lxiii. 9.

In that he is said to pity them, it is as much as to say he condoleth, feeleth, and sympathizeth with them in all their afflictions and temptations. So that this is the happiness of him that feareth God, he has a God to pity him, and to be touched with all his miseries. It is said, that "his soul was grieved for the misery of Israel," Judges x. 16. And in the Hebrews, he is said to be touched with the feeling of our infirmities, and can succour those that are tempted, Heb. iv. 15.

But further, let us take notice of the comparison. "As a father pitieth his children, so the Lord pitieth them that fear him." Here is not only pity, but the pity of a relation, a father. It is said, in another place, "Can a woman" (a mother) "forget her sucking child, that she should not have compassion on the son of her womb? Yea, they may forget, yet will I not forget thee," Isa. xlix. 15. The pity of neighbours and acquaintance helpeth in times of distress, but the pity of a father and a mother is pity with an over and above. "The Lord," says James, "is very pitiful, and of tender mercy," James v. 11. Pharaoh called Joseph his tender father, because he provided for him against the famine; but how tender a father is God! how full of bowels, how full of pity! It is said that when Ephraim was afflicted, God's bowels were troubled for him, and turned within him towards him. Oh that the man that feareth the Lord did but believe the pity and compassion that are in the heart of God and his Father towards him.

10. Dost thou fear God? "He will fulfil the desire of them that fear him: he also will hear their cry, and will save them," Psa. cxlv. 19.

Almost all those places that make mention of the

men that fear God, do intimate as if they still were under affliction, or in danger by reason of an enemy. But here is still their privilege, their God is their Father, and pities them.

" He will fulfil the desire of them that fear him." Where, now, is the man that feareth the Lord? let him hearken to this. What sayest thou, poor soul, will this content thee? The Lord will fulfil thy desires. It is intimated of Adonijah, that David his father did let him have his will in all things. " His father," says the text, " had not displeased him at any time in" so much as "saying, Why hast thou done so," 1 Kings i. 6. But here is more, here is a promise to grant thee the whole desire of thy heart, according to the prayer of holy David, the Lord " grant thee according to thine own heart, and fulfil all thy counsel." And again; "The Lord fulfil all thy petitions," Psa. xx. 4, 5.

O thou that fearest the Lord, what is thy desire? " All my desire," says David, " is all my salvation." So sayest thou, all my salvation is all my desire. Well, the desire of thy soul is granted thee, yea, God himself hath engaged himself even to fulfil this thy desire. " He will fulfil the desire of them that fear him : he also will hear their cry, and will save them." Oh this desire, when it cometh, what a tree of life will it be to thee! Thou desirest to be rid of thy present trouble; the Lord shall rid thee out of trouble. Thou desirest to be delivered from temptation; the Lord shall deliver thee out of temptation. Thou desirest to be delivered from thy body of death; and the Lord shall change this thy vile body, that it may be like to his glorious body, Phil. iii. 21. Thou desirest to be in the presence of God, and among the angels in heaven. This thy desire also shall be fulfilled, and thou shalt be made equal to the angels. Oh! but it is long first. Well, learn first to live upon thy portion in the promise of it, and that will make thy expectation of it sweet. God will fulfil thy desires. God will do it: though it tarry long, wait for it; because it will surely come, it will not tarry, Hab. ii. 3.

11. Dost thou fear God? "The Lord taketh pleasure in them that fear him," Psa. cxlvii. 11. Those that fear God are among his chief delights. He delights in his Son, he delights in his works, and takes pleasure in those that fear him. As a man takes pleasure in his wife, in his children, in his gold, in his jewels; so the man that fears the Lord is the object of his delight. He takes pleasure in their prosperity, and therefore sendeth them " health from the sanctuary," and makes them drink of the river of his pleasures. "They shall be abundantly satisfied with the fatness of thy house; and thou shalt make them drink of the river of thy pleasures," Psa. xxxvi. 8.

That or those we take pleasure in, we love to beautify and adorn with many ornaments. We count no cost too much to be bestowed on those in whom we place our delight, and whom we make the object of our pleasure. And even thus it is with God; "For the Lord taketh pleasure in his people :" and what follows? "He will beautify the meek with salvation," Psa. cxlix. 4.

Those in whom we delight, we take pleasure in their actions; yea, we teach them, and give them such rules and laws to walk by as may yet make those we love more pleasurable in our eyes.

Therefore those that fear God, since they are the objects of his pleasure, are taught to know how to please him in every thing. And hence it is said, that he is ravished with their looks, that he delighteth in their cry, and that he is pleased with their walking.

Those in whom we delight and take pleasure, many things we will bear and put up that they do, though they be not according to our minds. A man will suffer that in, and put up that at the hand of the child or wife of his pleasure, that he will not pass by nor put up in another.

God, speaking of his people, says, " They shall be mine, saith the Lord of hosts, in that day when I make up my jewels; and I will spare them, as a man spareth his own son that serveth him," Mal. iii. 17.

Oh, how happy is the man that feareth God! His good thoughts, his good attempts to serve him, and his good life, please him, because he feareth God.

You know how pleasing in our eyes the actions of our children are, when we know that they do what they do even of a reverential fear and awe of us; yea, though that which they do amounts but to little, we take it well at their hands, and are pleased therewith. The woman that cast in her two mites into the treasury cast in not much, for they did but make one farthing; yet how doth the Lord Jesus trumpet her up. He had pleasure in her and in her action. This, therefore, that the Lord taketh pleasure in those that fear him, is another of their great privileges.

12. Dost thou fear God? The least portion of that fear giveth the privilege to be blessed with the

greatest saint. "He will bless them that fear the
Lord, both small and great," Psa. cxv. 13. This
word small may be taken three ways :—

(1.) For those that are small in esteem ; for those
that are but little accounted of, Judges vi. 15. Art
thou small or little in this sense, yet, if thou fearest
God, thou art sure to be blessed. "He will bless
them that fear the Lord, both small and great." Be
thou never so small in the world's eyes, in thine own
eyes, in the saints' eyes, (as sometimes one saint is
little in another saint's eye,) yet thou, because thou
fearest God, art put among the blessed.

(2.) By small, sometimes, is meant those that are
but small of stature, or young in years, little children, that are easily passed by and looked over ; as
those that sang hosanna in the temple were, when
the Pharisees deridingly said of them to Christ,
"Hearest thou what these say ?" Matt. xxi. 16.
Well, but Christ would not despise those children
that feared God, but preferred them, by the Scripture testimony, far before those that did contemn
them. Little children, how small soever, and although of never so small esteem with men, shall
also, if they fear the Lord, be blessed with the
greatest saints. "He shall bless them that fear
the Lord, both small and great."

(3.) By small may, sometimes, be meant those
that are small in grace or gifts. These are said to be
the least in the church, that is, under this consideration, and so are by it least esteemed. Thus also is
that word of Christ to be understood, "Inasmuch
as ye did it not to one of the least of these, ye did it
not to me," Matt. xxv. 45.

Art thou, in thine own thoughts, or in the thoughts
of others, of these last small ones ? small in grace,

small in gifts, small in esteem upon this account;
yet if thou fearest God, if thou fearest God indeed,
thou art certainly blest with the best of saints. The
least star stands as fixed as the biggest of them all
in heaven. "He shall bless them that fear him,
both small and great." He shall bless them; that
is, with the same blessing of eternal life: for the
different degrees of grace in saints doth not make the
blessing, as to its nature, differ. It is the same
heaven, the same life, the same glory, and the same
eternity of felicity that they are, in the text, promised
to be blessed with. That is observable which I
mentioned before, where Christ, at the day of judgment, particularly mentions and owns the least:
"Inasmuch as ye did it not to one of the least."
The least, then, were there, in his kingdom and in his
glory, as well as the biggest of all.

"He shall bless them that fear him, both small and
great." The small are named first in the text, and
are so the first in rank, it may be to show, that though
they may be slighted, and little set by in the world,
yet they are much set by in the eyes of the Lord.

Are great saints only to have the kingdom and the
glory everlasting? Are great works only to be rewarded? works that are done by virtue of great
grace and the abundance of the gifts of the Holy
Ghost? No; "Whosoever shall give to drink unto
one of these little ones a cup of cold water only in
the name of a disciple, verily I say unto you, He shall
in no wise lose his reward," Matt. x. 42. Mark,
here is but a little gift, a cup of cold water, and that
given to a little saint, but both taken special notice
of by our Lord Jesus Christ. He will give reward
to his servants the prophets, and to his saints, and to
those that fear his name, small and great, Rev. xi. 18.

The small, therefore, among those that fear God, are blessed with the great, and as the great, with the same salvation, the same glory, and the same eternal life; and they shall have, even as the great ones also shall, as much as they can carry, as much as their hearts, souls, bodies, and capacities can hold.

13. Dost thou fear God? Why, the Holy Ghost hath on purpose indited for thee a whole psalm to sing concerning thyself; so that thou mayest, even as thou art in thy calling, bed, journey, or wherever, sing out thine own blessed and happy condition to thine own comfort, and the comfort of thy fellows. The psalm is the 128th. I will set it before thee:—

"Blessed is every one that feareth the Lord; that walketh in his ways. For thou shalt eat the labour of thine hands: happy shalt thou be, and it shall be well with thee. Thy wife shall be as a fruitful vine by the sides of thine house : thy children like olive plants round about thy table. Behold, that thus shall the man be blessed that feareth the Lord. The Lord shall bless thee out of Zion: and thou shalt see the good of Jerusalem all the days of thy life. Yea, thou shalt see thy children's children, and peace upon Israel."

And now I have done with the privileges when I have removed one objection.

Object. But the Scripture says, "Perfect love casteth out fear," 1 John iv. 18, and therefore it seems that saints, after that the Spirit of adoption is come, should not fear, but do their duty, as another Scripture saith, "without fear," Luke i. 74.

Ans. Fear, as I have showed you, may be taken several ways.

(1) It may be taken for the fear of devils.

(2.) It may be taken for the fear of reprobates.

(3.) It may be taken for the fear that is wrought in the godly, by the Spirit as a Spirit of bondage. Or,

(4.) It may be taken for the fear that I have been but now discoursing of.

Now, the fear that perfect love casts out cannot be that sunlike, gracious fear of God that I have in this last place been treating of; because that fear which love casts out hath torment; but so has not the sonlike fear. Therefore, the fear which love casts out is either that fear which is like the fear of devils and reprobates, or that fear which is begot in the heart by the Spirit of God as a Spirit of bondage, or both; for indeed all these kinds of fear have torment, and therefore may be cast out, and are so by the Spirit of adoption, which is called the Spirit of faith and love, when he comes with power into the soul. So that, without this fear we should serve him.

But to argue from these texts that we ought not to fear God, or to mix fear with our worship of him, is as much as to say that by the Spirit of adoption we are brought under condemnation, for he that does not fear God is in such a state. But for what I have affirmed the Scripture doth plentifully confirm, saying, "Happy is the man that feareth alway," Prov. xxviii. 14. And again, "It shall be well with them that fear God, which fear before him," Eccles. viii. 12.

The fear of the Lord, therefore, is a grace that greatly beautifies a Christian, his words, and all his ways. "Wherefore now let the fear of the Lord be upon you; take heed and do it: for there is no iniquity with the Lord our God, nor respect of persons, nor taking of gifts," 2 Chron. xix. 7.

CHAPTER VI.

THE USE OF THIS DOCTRINE.

HAVING proceeded thus far about this doctrine of the fear of God, I now come to make some use and application of the whole; and my first use shall be a use of examination.

I. Is this fear of God such an excellent thing? Is it attended with so many blessed privileges, then this should put us, every soul of us, upon a diligent examination of ourselves, namely, whether this grace be in us or not; for if it be, then thou art one of these blessed ones to whom belong these glorious privileges, for thou hast an interest in every one of them. But if it shall appear that this grace is not in thee, then thy state is fearfully miserable, as hath partly been manifest already, and will further be seen in what comes after.

Now, the better to help thee to consider, and not to miss in finding out what thou art, in thy self-examination, I will speak to this,

1. In general.
2. In particular.

1. In general. No man brings this grace into the world with him. Every one by nature is destitute of it, for naturally none fear God; "There is no fear of God," none of this grace of fear, "before their eyes," Rom. iii. 18; they do not so

much as know what it is; for this fear flows, as was shown before, from a new heart, faith, repentance, and the like; of which new heart, faith, and repentance, if thou art void, thou art also void of this godly fear. Men must have a mighty change of heart and life, or else they are strangers to this fear of God. Alas, how ignorant are the most of this! Yea, and some are not afraid to say they are not changed, nor desire so to be. Can these fear God? Can these be possessed with this grace of fear? No; because they have no changes, therefore they fear not God, Psa. lv. 19.

Wherefore, sinner, consider, whoever thou art, that art destitute of this fear of God, thou art void of all other graces; for this fear, as I have shown, floweth from the whole stock of grace where it is. There is not one of the graces of the Spirit, but this fear is in it; yea, as I may say, this fear is the flower and beauty of every grace, neither is there anything, let it look as much like grace as it will, that will be counted so indeed, if the fruit thereof be not this fear of God. Wherefore, I say again, consider well of this matter, for as thou shall be found with reference to this grace, so shall thy judgment be. I have but briefly treated of this grace, yet have endeavoured, with words as fit as I could, to display it in its colours before thy face; first, by showing you what this fear of God is, then what it flows from, as also what doth flow from it; to which, as was said before, I have added several privileges that are annexed to this fear, that by all, if it may be, thou mayest see it, if thou hast it, and thyself without it, if thou hast it not. Wherefore, I refer thee thither again for information in this thing. Or, if thou art loth to give the book a second reading, but wilt go on to the end now thou art got hither, then,

2. Secondly, and particularly, I conclude with these several propositions concerning those that fear not God.

(1.) That man that is proud, and of an high and lofty mind, fears not God. This is plain from the exhortation, "Be not highminded, but fear," Rom. xi. 20. Here you see that a high mind and the fear of God are set in direct opposition the one to the other, and there is in them, closely concluded by the apostle, that where indeed the one is there cannot be the other; where there is a high mind, there is not the fear of God, and where there is the fear of God, the mind is not high, but lowly. Can a man at the same time be a proud man and fear God too? Why then is it said, God beholdeth every one that is proud, and abases him; and again, that he beholds the proud afar off? Job xl. 11; Psa. cxxxviii. 6.

He, therefore, that is proud of his person, of his riches, of his office, of his parts, and the like, feareth not God. It is also manifest further, for "God resisteth the proud," James iv. 6, which he would not do if he feared him; but in that he sets him at such a distance from him, in that he testifies that he will abase him and resist him, it is evident that he is not the man that hath this grace of fear; for that man, as I have showed you, is the man of God's delight, the object of his pleasure.

(2.) The covetous man feareth not God. This also is plain from the word, because it setteth covetousness and the fear of God in direct opposition. Men that fear God are said to hate covetousness, Exod. xviii. 21. Besides, the covetous man is called an idolater, and is said to have no part in the kingdom of Christ and of God, Col. iii. 5. And again; "The wicked boasteth of his heart's desire, and blesseth the covetous, whom the Lord abhorreth," Psa. x. 3.

Hearken to this, you that hunt the world to take it, you that care not how you get, so you get the world; also, you that make even religion your stalking-horse to get the world. You fear not God. And what will you do, whose hearts go after your covetousness? you who are led by covetousness up and down, as it were by the nose; sometimes to swear, to lie, to cozen, and cheat and defraud, when you can get the advantage to do it. You are far, very far from the fear of God. "Ye adulterers and adulteresses," for so the covetous are called, "know ye not that the friendship of the world is enmity with God? whosoever therefore will be a friend of the world is the enemy of God," James iv. 4.

(3.) The riotous eaters of flesh have not the fear of God; for this is done without fear, Jude 12. Gluttony is a sin little taken notice of, and as little repented of by those that use it; but yet it is odious in the sight of God, and the practice of it a demonstration of the want of his fear in the heart; yea, so odious is it, that God forbids that his people should so much as company with such. "Be not," saith he, "among wine-bibbers; among riotous eaters of flesh," Prov. xxiii. 20. And he further tells us, that those that are such are spots and blemishes to those that keep them company, for indeed they fear not God, 2 Peter ii. 13.

Alas! some men are as if they were born for nought else but to eat, and to drink, and pamper their carcasses with the dainties of this world, quite forgetting why God sent them hither; but such, as is said, fear not God, and so, consequently, are of the

number of those upon whom the day of judgment
will come unawares, Luke xxi. 34.

(4.) The liar is one that fears not God. This also
is evident from a plain text; "Thou hast lied, and
hast not remembered me, nor laid it to thy heart;
have not I held my peace even of old, and thou
fearest me not?" Isa. lvii. 11. What lie this was is
not material; it was a lie, or a course of lying, that
is here rebuked, and the person or persons in this
practice, as is said, were such as feared not God; a
course of lying and the fear of God cannot stand
together.

This sin of lying is a common sin, and it walketh
in the world in several guises. There is the profane
scoffing liar; there is the cunning artificial liar; there
is the hypocritical religious liar; with liars of other
ranks and degrees; but none of them all have the
fear of God, nor shall any of them, except they repent, escape the damnation of hell. "All liars shall
have their part in the lake which burneth with fire
and brimstone," Rev. xxi. 8. Heaven and the new
Jerusalem are not a place for such: "And there
shall in no wise enter into it any thing that defileth,
neither whatsoever worketh abomination, or maketh
a lie," ver. 27. Therefore another scripture says,
"Without are dogs, and sorcerers, and whoremon-
gers, and murderers, and idolaters, and whosoever
loveth and maketh a lie," chap. xxii. 15. But this
should not be their sentence, judgment, and condemnation, if those that are liars were such as had
in them this blessed fear of God.

(5.) Those fear not God who cry unto him for help
in the time of their calamity, and when they are delivered return to their former rebellion. Moses, in a
spirit of prophecy, asserteth this, at the time of the

mighty judgment of the hail. Pharaoh then desired
him to pray to God that he would take away that
judgment from him. Well, so I will, said Moses,
"but as for thee and thy servants, I know that ye
will not fear the Lord God," Exod. ix. 30. As if he
should say, I know that so soon as this judgment is
removed, you will go to your old rebellion again.
And what greater demonstration can be given that
such a man feareth not God, than to cry to God to
be delivered from affliction to prosperity, and to
spend that prosperity in rebellion against him?
This is crying for mercies that they may be spent,
or that we may have something to spend, upon our
lusts, and in the service of Satan, James iv. 3.

Of these God complains in Ezekiel; "Thou hast
also taken thy fair jewels of my gold and of my
silver, which I had given thee, and madest to thyself images of men, and didst commit whoredom
with them," Ezek. xvi. 17.

This was for want of the fear of God. Many of
this kind there be now in the world, both of men, and
women, and children. Art not thou that readest
this book of this number? Hast thou not cried for
health when sick, for wealth when poor, when lame
for strength, when in prison for liberty, and then
spent all that thou gottest by thy prayer in the
service of Satan, and to gratify thy lusts? Look to
it, sinner, these things are signs that with thy heart
thou fearest not God.

(6.) Those fear not God that waylay his people,
and seek to overthrow them, or to turn them besides
the right path, as they are journeying from hence to
their eternal rest. This is evident from the plain
text, "Remember what Amalek did unto thee by
the way, when ye were come forth out of Egypt;

how he met thee by the way, and smote the hindmost of thee, even all that were feeble behind thee, when thou wast faint and weary; and he feared not God," Deut. xxv. 17, 18.

Many such Amalekites there be now in the world, that have set themselves against the feeble of the flock especially, still smiting them, some by power, some with the tongue, some in their lives and estates, some in their names and reputations, by scandal, slanders, and reproach; but the reason of this their ungodly practice is this, they fear not God; for did they fear him they would be afraid to so much as think, much more of attempting to afflict and destroy, and calumniate the children of God: but such there have been, such there are, and such there will be in the world, for all men fear not God.

(7.) Those fear not God who see his hand upon backsliders for their sins, and yet themselves will be backsliders also. "I saw," saith God, "when for all the causes whereby backsliding Israel committed adultery I had put her away, and given her a bill of divorce; yet her treacherous sister Judah feared not, but went and played the harlot also," Jer. iii. 8.

Judah saw that her sister was put away, and delivered by God into the hand of Salmanezer, who carried her away beyond Babylon; and yet, though she saw it, she went and played the harlot also, a sign of great hardness of heart, and of the want of the fear of God indeed; for his fear, had it been in her heart, would have taught her to have trembled at the judgment that was executed upon her sister, and not to have gone and played the harlot also; and not to have done it while her sister's judgment was in sight and memory. But what is it that a heart that is destitute of the fear of God will not do? No sin comes amiss to such; yea, they will sin, they will do that themselves, for the doing of which they be-believe some are in hell-fire, and all because they fear not God.

But pray observe, if those that take not warning, when they see the hand of God upon backsliders, are said to have none of the fear of God, have those it, think you, that lay stumbling-blocks in the way of God's people, and use devices to cause them to backslide, yea, rejoice when they can do this mis-chief to any? And yet many of this sort there are in the world, that even rejoice when they see a pro-fessor fall into sin, and go back from his profession, as if they had found some excellent thing.

(8.) Those fear not God who can look upon a land wallowing in sin, and yet are not humbled at the sight thereof. "Have ye forgotten," said God, by the prophet, to the Jews, " the wickedness of your fathers, and the wickedness of the kings of Judah, and the wickedness of their wives, and your own wickedness, and the wickedness of your wives, which they have committed in the land of Judah, and in the streets of Jerusalem? 'They are not humbled even unto this day, neither have they feared, nor walked in my law," Jer. xliv. 9, 10.

Here was a land full of wickedness, and none to bewail it, for they wanted the fear of God, and love to walk in his law. But how say you, if those that are not humbled at their own and others' wicked-ness are said not to fear, or have the fear of God, what shall we think or say of such that receive, that nourish, and rejoice in such wickedness? Do they . fear God? Yea, what shall we say of such that are the inventors and promoters of wickedness, as of

oaths, beastly talk, or the like ? ·Do you think they
fear God ?

Once again ; what shall we say of such that cannot
be content to be wicked themselves, and to invent
and rejoice in other men's wickedness, but must
hate, reproach, vilify, and abuse those that they
cannot persuade to be wicked ?   Do they fear God ?

(9.) Those that take more heed to their own dreams
than to the word of God, fear not God. This also is
plain from the word ; " For in the multitude of
dreams and many words there are also divers vani-
ties : but fear thou God ;" that is, take heed unto his
word, Eccles. v. 7.

Here the fearing of God is opposed to our over-
much heeding dreams ; and it is implied, that it
is for want of the fear of God that men so much
heed those things.

What will those say to this that give more heed to
a suggestion which ariseth from their foolish hearts,
or that is cast in thither by the devil, than they do
to the holy word of God ?   These are " filthy
dreamers," Jude 8.

Also, what shall we say to those that are more
confident of the mercy of God to their souls, because
he hath blessed them with outward things, than they
are afraid of his wrath and condemnation, though
the whole of the word of God doth fully verify the
same ?   These are filthy dreamers indeed.

A dream is either real, or so by way of semblance ;
and so some men dream sleeping, and some waking.
And as those that a man dreams sleeping are caused
either by God, Satan, business, the flesh, or the like,
so are those that a man dreams waking, to pass by
those that we have in our sleep.

Men, when bodily awake, may have dreams, that is, visions from heaven ; such are all they that have a tendency to discover to the sinner his state, or the state of the church according to the word.

But those that are from Satan, business, and the flesh are such, (especially the first and last, namely, from Satan and the flesh,) as tend to embolden men to hope for good in a way disagreeing with the word of God. These Jude calls " filthy dreamers," such whose principles were their dreams, and they led them to defile the flesh, that is, by fornication and uncleanness ; to " despise dominion," that the reins might be laid upon the neck of their lusts ; to " speak evil of dignities," of those that God had set over them, for their governing in all the law and testament of Christ : these dreamed that to live like brutes, to be greedy of gain, and to take away for it, as Cain and Balaam did by their wiles, the lives of the owners thereof, would go for good coin in the best of trials. These also Peter speaks of, 2 Pet. ii. And he makes their dreams, that Jude so calls, their principles and errors in life and doctrine. You may read of them in that whole chapter, where they are called " cursed children ;" and so, by consequence, such as fear not God.

(10.) Those fear not God who are sorcerers, adulterers, false swearers, and that oppress the hireling of his wages.

It is a custom with some men to keep back, by fraud, from the hireling that which by covenant they agreed to pay for their labour ; pinching, I say, and paring from them their due which of right belongs to them, to the making of them cry in the ears of the Lord of sabaoth, James v. 4. These fear not God ; they are reckoned among the worst of men, and in their day of account God himself will bear witness against them. "And I will come near to you to judgment; and I will be a swift witness against the sorcerers, and against the adulterers, and against false swearers, and against those that oppress the hireling in his wages, the widow, and the fatherless, and that turn aside the stranger from his right, and fear not me, saith the Lord," Mal. iii. 5.

(11.) Those fear not God who, instead of pitying, rail at God's people in their afflictions, temptations, and persecutions, and rather rejoice and skip for joy, than sympathize with them in their sorrow. Thus did David's enemies, thus did Israel's enemies, and thus did the thief; he railed at Christ when he hanged upon the cross, and was for that, even by his fellow, accounted for one that feared not God, Luke xxiii. 40.

This is a common thing among the children of men, even to rejoice at the hurt of those that fear God, and it ariseth even of an inward hatred to godliness. They hate you, says Christ, because they hated me, John xv. 18. Therefore Christ takes what is done to his, in this, as done unto himself, and so to holiness of life.

But this falls hard upon such as despise, and rejoice to see God's people in their griefs, and that take the advantage, as dogged Shimei did, to augment the griefs and afflictions of God's people, 2 Sam. xvi. 5—8.

(12.) Those fear not God who are strangers to the effects of fear. "If I be a master, where is my fear?" Mal. i. 6. That is, show that I am so by your fear of me, in the effects of your fear of me. "You offer polluted bread upon mine altar," ver. 7. This is not a sign that you fear me; ye offer the blind for sacrifices, where is my fear? Ye offer the lame and the sick; these are not effects of the fear of God, ver. 8.

Sinner, it is one thing to say, I fear God, and another to fear him indeed. Therefore James says, "I will show thee my faith by my works," Jam. ii. 18, so here God calls for a testimony of thy fear by the effects of fear. I have already showed you several effects of fear; if thou art a stranger to them, thou art a stranger to this grace of fear. Therefore, to conclude this, it is not a feigned profession that will do; nothing is good here but what is salted with this fear of God; and those that fear him are men of truth, men of singleness of heart, perfect, upright, humble, holy men. Wherefore, reader, examine, and again I say, examine, and lay the word and thy heart together before thou concludest that thou fearest God.

What! fear God, and in a state of nature! Fear God without a change of heart and life! What! fear God, and be proud and covetous, a wine bibber, and a riotous eater of flesh! How! fear God, and a liar, and one that cries for mercies to spend them upon thy lusts! this would be strange.

True, thou mayest fear as devils do, but what will that profit? Thou mayest, by thy fear, be driven away from God, from his worship, people, and ways; but what will that avail? It may be thou mayest so fear at present as to be a little stopped in thy sinful course. Perhaps thou hast got a reproof from the word of God, and art at present a little hindered from thy former and full career after sin; but what of that? If by the fear that thou hast, thy heart is not united to God and to the love of his Son, word, and people, thy fear is nothing worth.

Many men also are forced to fear God the same as

underlings are forced to fear those that are by force above them.

If thou only thus fearest God, it is but a false fear; it flows not from love to God. This fear brings not willing subjection, which indeed brings the effect of right fear; but being overmastered, like an hypocrite, thou subjectest thyself by feigned obedience, being forced, I say, by mere dread to do it, Psa. lxvi. 3.

It is said, "The fame of David went out into all lands; and the Lord brought the fear of him upon all nations," 1 Chron. xiv. 17. But what did they now love David? Did they now choose him to be their king? No, verily; many of them rather hated him; and when they could, made resistance against him. They did even as thou dost; they feared, but did not love; feared, but did not choose his government that ruled over them.

It is also said of Jehoshaphat, when God had subdued before him Ammon, Moab, and Mount Seir, that "the fear of God was on all the kingdoms of those countries, when they heard that the Lord fought against the enemies of Israel," 2 Chron. xx. 29. But, I say, was this fear, that is called now the fear of God, anything else but a dread of the greatness and power of the king? No, verily, nor did that dread bring them into a willing subjection to, and liking of his laws and government; it only made them, like slaves and underlings, stand in fear of his executing the vengeance of God upon them.

Therefore, notwithstanding this fear, they were rebels to him in their hearts, and when occasion and advantage offered themselves, they showed it by rising in rebellion against Israel.

This fear, therefore, provoked but feigned and

forced obedience; a right emblem of the obedience of such who, being still enemies in their minds to God, are forced, by virtue of present conviction, to yield a little, even of fear to God, to his word, and to his ordinances. Reader, whoever thou art, think of this, it is thy concern, therefore do it; and examine, and examine again, and look diligently to thy heart in thine examination, that it beguile thee not about this thy so great concern, as indeed the fear of God is.

One thing more let me warn thee of before I leave thee. Take heed of deferring to fear the Lord. Some men, when they have had conviction upon their heart that the fear of God is not in them, have, through the overpowering of their corruptions, yet deferred and put off the fear of God from them, as it is said of those in Jeremiah, "This people hath a revolting and a rebellious heart; they are revolted and gone: neither say they in their heart, Let us now fear the Lord," Jer. v. 23, 24.

They saw that the judgments of God attended them, because they did not yet fear God; but that conviction would not prevail with them to say, Let us now fear the Lord. They were for deferring to fear him still; they were for putting off his fear from them longer. Sinner, hast thou deferred to fear the Lord? Is thy heart still so stubborn as not yet to say, " Let us fear the Lord?" Oh, the Lord hath taken notice of this thy rebellion, and is preparing some dreadful judgment for thee. "Shall I not visit for these things? saith the Lord: shall not my soul be avenged on such a nation as this?" ver. 29.

Sinner, why shouldst thou pull vengeance down from heaven upon thee? Look up; perhaps thou hast already been pulling this great while, to pull it down upon thee. Oh, pull no longer. Why shouldst

thou be thine own executioner? Fall down upon
thy knees, man, and up with thy heart and thy
hands to the God that dwells in the heavens; cry,
yea, cry aloud, "Lord, unite mine heart to fear thy
name, and do not harden mine heart from thy fear."
Thus holy men have cried before thee, and by crying have prevented judgment.

Before I leave this use, let me give thee a few
things that, if God will, may provoke thee to fear
the Lord.

The man that feareth not God carrieth it worse
toward him than the beast, the brute beast doth
carry it towards that man. "The fear of you and
the dread of you shall be upon every beast of the
earth, and upon every fowl of the air, upon all that
moveth upon the earth, and upon all the fishes in
the sea," Gen. ix. 2.

Mark, all my creatures shall fear you, and dread
you, says God. None of them shall be so hardy
as to cast off all reverence of you. But what a
shame is this to man, that God should subject
all his creatures to him, and he should refuse to
stoop his heart to God! The beast, the bird, the
fish, and all, have a fear and dread of man, yea God
has put it in their hearts to fear a man, and yet man
is void of fear and dread, I mean of godly fear, of
Him, that thus lovingly hath put all things under
him. Sinner! art thou not ashamed that a silly
cow, a sheep, yea, swine, should better observe
the law of creation than thou dost the law of thy
God?

Consider, he that will not fear God, God will
make him fear him whether he will or not. That is,
he that doth not, will not now so fear him, as
willingly to bow before him, and put his neck into

his yoke, God will make him fear him when he comes to take vengeance on him. Then he will surround him with terror, and with fear on every side; fear within, and fear without; fear shall be in the way, even in the way that thou goest when thou art going out of this world; and that will be dreadful fear. God says, " I will choose their delusions, and will bring their fears upon them," Isa. lxvi. 4.

He that fears not God now, the Lord shall laugh at his fears then. Sinner, God will be even with all those that choose not to have his fear in their hearts; for as he calls, and they hear not now, so they shall cry, yea howl then, and he will laugh at their fears. "I will laugh," saith he, "at your calamity; I will mock when your fear cometh; when your fear cometh as desolation, and your destruction cometh as a whirlwind; when distress and anguish cometh upon you. Then shall they call upon me, but I will not answer; they shall seek me early, but they shall not find me : for that they hated knowledge, and did not choose the fear of the Lord," Prov. i. 26—29.

Sinner! thou thinkest to escape the fear; but what wilt thou do with the pit? Thou thinkest to escape the pit; but what wilt thou do with the snare. The snare, say you, what is that? I answer, it is even the work of thine own hands. "The wicked is snared in the work of his own hands," Psa. ix. 16. "The wicked is snared by the transgression of his lips," Prov. xii. 13.

Sinner! what wilt thou do when thou comest into this snare; that is, into the guilt and terror that thy sins will bind thee with, when they, like a cord, are fastened about thy soul? This snare will bring thee back again to the pit, which is hell; and then,

N

how wilt thou do to be rid of thy fear? The fear,
pit, and the snare shall come upon thee, because
thou fearest not God.

Sinner! art thou one of those that hast cast off
fear? Poor man, what wilt thou do when these
three things beset thee? Whither wilt thou flee for
help, and where wilt thou leave thy glory? If thou
fleest from the fear, there is the pit; if thou fleest
from the pit, there is the snare.

II. The second use is an exhortation to fear God.

My next word shall be an exhortation to fear God;
I mean an exhortation to saints. "O fear the Lord,
ye his saints: for there is no want to them that fear
him," Psa. xxxiv. 9.

Not but that every saint doth fear God; but, as the
apostle saith in another case, "I beseech you that ye
would abound more and more," 1 Thess. iv. 1. The
fear of the Lord, as I have showed you, is a grace of
the new covenant, as other saving graces are, and so
is capable of being stronger or weaker, as other
graces are. Wherefore, I beseech you, fear him
more and more.

It is said of Obadiah, that he " feared the Lord
greatly." Every saint fears the Lord, but every saint
does not greatly fear him. Oh there are but few Oba-
diahs in the world; I mean among the saints on earth:
see the whole relation of him, 1 Kings xviii. As Paul
said of Timothy, " I have no man likeminded," Phil.
ii. 20; so it may be said of some concerning the fear
of the Lord; they have scarcely an equal. So it was
with Job; "There is none like him in the earth, a
perfect and an upright man, one that feareth God,
and escheweth evil," Job i. 8. There was even no
one in Job's day that feared God like him; no, there
was not one like him in all the earth: but doubtless

there were more in the world that feared God; but
this fearing of him greatly, that is the thing that
saints should do, and that was the thing that Job did
do, and in that he did outstrip his fellows.

It is also said of Hananiah, that "he was a
faithful man, and feared God above many," Neh.
vii. 2. He also had got, as to the exercise of, and
growth in this grace, the start of many of his
brethren. He "feared God above many." Now
then, seeing this grace admits of degrees, and is in
some stronger, and in some weaker, let us be all
awakened, as to other graces, so to this grace also;
that like as you "abound in every thing, in faith, and
utterance, and knowledge, and in all diligence, and
in your love to us, see that ye abound in this grace
also," 2 Cor. viii. 7.

I will labour to enforce this exhortation upon you
by several motives.

1. Let God's distinguishing love to you be a motive
to you to fear him greatly. He hath put his fear in
thy heart, and hath not given that blessing to thy
neighbour; perhaps not to thy husband, thy wife,
thy child, or thy parent. Oh, what an obligation
should this consideration lay upon thy heart greatly
to fear the Lord! Remember, also, that this fear of
the Lord is his treasure, a choice jewel, given only
to favourites, and to those that are greatly beloved.

Great gifts naturally tend to oblige, and will do
so, I trust, with thee, when thou shalt ingenuously
consider it. It is a sign of a very bad nature when
the contrary shows itself. Could God have done
more for thee than to have put his fear in thy heart?
This is better than to have given thee a place even
in heaven without it. Yea, had he given thee all
faith, all knowledge, and the tongue of men and

N 2

angels, and a place in heaven to boot, they had all been short of this gift, of the fear of God in thy heart. Therefore love it, nourish it, exercise it, use all means to cause it to increase and grow in thy heart, that it may appear it is set by at thy hand, poor sinner.

(2.) Another motive to stir thee up to grow in this grace of the fear of God, may be the privileges that it lays thee under. What, or where wilt thou find in the Bible so many privileges, so affectionately entailed to any grace, as to this of the fear of God? God speaks of this grace, and of the privileges that belong unto it, as if (to speak with reverence) he knew not how to have done blessing of the man that hath it.

It seems to me, as if this grace of fear is the darling grace, the grace that God sets his heart upon at the highest rate. As it were, he embraces, and lays the man in his bosom, that hath and grows strong in this grace of the fear of God.

See again, the many privileges in which the man is interested that hath this grace in his heart; and see also that there are but few of them, wherever mentioned, but have entailed to them the pronunciation of a blessing, or else that man is spoken of by way of admiration.

(3.) Another motive may be this: the man that groweth in this grace of the fear of the Lord, will escape those evils that others will fall into. Where this grace is, it keepeth the soul from final apostasy. " I will put my fear in their hearts, that they shall not depart from me," Jer. xxxii. 40. But yet if there be not an increase in this grace, much evil may attend and be committed notwithstanding.

There is a child that is healthy, and hath its limbs, and can go; but it is careless. Now, the evil of carelessness doth disadvantage it very much; carelessness is the cause of stumblings, of falls, and that it falls into the dirt, yea, that sometimes it is burned, or almost drowned. And thus it is even with God's people that fear him, because they add not to their fear a care of growing more in the fear of God, therefore they reap damage: whereas, were they more in his fear, it would keep them better, deliver them more, and preserve them from these snares of death.

(4.) Another motive may be this: to grow in this grace of the fear of God, is the way to be kept always in a conscientious performance of Christian duties.

An increase in this grace, I say, keeps every grace in exercise, and the keeping of our graces in their due exercise, produceth a conscientious performance of duties. Thou hast a watch, perhaps, in thy pocket, but the hand will not as yet be kept in any good order, but does always give thee the lie as to the hour of the day: well, what is the way to remedy this but to look well to the spring and the wheels within; for if they indeed go right, so will the hand do also. This is thy case in spiritual things. Thou art a gracious man, and the fear of God is in thee; but yet, for all that, one cannot well tell by thy life what time a day it is. Thou givest no true and constant sign that thou art indeed a Christian. Why the reason is, thou dost not look well to this grace of the fear of God; thou dost not grow and increase in that, but sufferest thy heart to grow careless and hard, and so thy life remiss and worldly. Job's growing great in the fear of God made him eschew evil.

(5.) Another motive is: this is the way to be wise indeed. "A wise man feareth, and departeth from evil," Prov. xiv. 16. It doth not say a wise man hath the grace of fear, but a wise man feareth, that is, putteth this grace into exercise. There is no greater sign of wisdom than to grow in this blessed grace. Is it not a sign of wisdom to depart from sins which are the snares of death and hell? Is it not a sign of wisdom for a man yet more and more to endeavour to interest himself in the love and protection of God? Is it not a high point of wisdom for a man to be always doing that which lays him under the conduct of angels? Surely this is wisdom? And if it be a blessing to have this fear, is it not wisdom to increase in it? Doubtless it is the highest point of wisdom, as I have shown before; therefore grow therein.

(6.) Another motive may be this: it is seemly for saints to fear, and increase in this fear of God.

He is thy Creator? Is it not seemly for creatures to fear and reverence their Creator? He is thy King. Is it not seemly for subjects to fear and reverence their king? He is thy Father. Is it not seemly for children · to reverence and fear their father? yea, and to do it more and more?

(7.) Another motive may be: it is honourable to grow in this grace of fear. "When Ephraim spake trembling, he exalted himself in Israel," Hos. xiii. 1.

Truly to fear, and to abound in this fear, is a sign of a very princely spirit; and the reason is, when I greatly fear my God, I am above the fear of all others, nor can any thing in this world, be it never so terrible and dreadful, move me at all to fear them. And hence it is that Christ counsels us to fear: "And I say unto you, my friends, Be not afraid of them that kill the body, and after that have no more that they can do. But I will forewarn you

whom ye shall fear: Fear him, which after he hath
killed hath power to cast into hell ; yea, I say unto
you, Fear him," Luke xii. 4, 5.

Indeed, this true fear of God sets a man above all
the world ; and therefore it is said again, " Neither
fear ye their fear, nor be afraid.   Sanctify the Lord
of hosts himself; and let him be your fear, and let
him be your dread," Isa. viii. 12, 13.

Your ranting boasters, that are ignorant of the
·nature of this fear of God, count it a poor sneaking,
pitiful, cowardly spirit in men to fear and tremble
before the Lord ; but whoso looks back to gaols,
and gibbets, to the sword and burning stake, shall
see that there has been seen the most mighty and
invincible spirit that has been in the world.

Yea, see if God doth not count that the growth of
his people in this grace of fear is that which makes
them honourable, when he excludeth those from a
dwelling place in his house that do not honour them
that fear him.   And he saith, moreover, "A woman
that feareth the Lord, she shall be praised," Prov.
xxxi. 30.   If the world and godless men will not
honour these, they shall be honoured some way else.
"Them," saith he, "that honour me, I will honour," 1 Sam. ii. 30 ; and they shall be honoured in
heaven, in the churches, and among the angels.

(8.) Another motive to grow in this fear of God
may be : this fear, and the increase of it, qualifies a
man to be put in trust with heavenly and spiritual
things, yea, and with earthly things to.

For heavenly and spiritual things.   " My covenant," saith God, " was with him of life and peace ;
and I gave them to him for the fear wherewith he
feared me, and was afraid before my name," Mal. ii. 5.
Behold what a gift, what a mercy, what a blessing

this Levi is intrusted with; namely, with God's everlasting covenant, and with the life and peace that are
wrapped up in this covenant!   But why is it given
to him ?   The answer is, " For the fear wherewith
he feared me, and was afraid before my name."
And the reason is good ; for this fear of God teaches
a man to put a due estimation upon every gift of
God bestowed upon us ; also, it teaches us to make
use of the same with reverence of his name, and
respect to his glory in most godly-wise, all which
becomes him that is intrusted with any spiritual
gift.   The gift here was given to Levi to minister
to his brethren doctrinally thereof, for he, saith God,
shall teach Jacob my statutes and Israel my law,
Deut. xxxiii. 10.

See also Exod. xviii. 21, and Nehem. vii. 2, with
many other places that might be named, and you
will find, that men fearing God, and hating covetousness, that men that fear God above others, are intrusted by God, yea, and by his church too, with the
trust and ministration of spiritual things before any
other in the world.

For earthly things.   This fear of God qualifies a
man to be put in trust with them rather than with
another.   Therefore God made Joseph lord of all
Egypt; Obadiah, steward of Ahab's house ; Daniel,
Mordecai, and the three children, were set over the
province of Babylon ;   and this by the wonderful
working hand of God, because he had to dispose of
earthly things now, not only in a common way, but
for the good of his people in special.   True, when
there is no special matter, or thing to be done by
God in a nation for his people, then who will, that
is, whether they have grace or not, may have the disposal of those things ; but if God has any thing in

special to bestow upon his people of this world's good, then he will intrust it in the hands of men fearing God. Joseph must now be made lord of Egypt, because Israel must be kept from starving; Obadiah must now be made steward of Ahab's house, because the Lord's prophets must be hid from, and fed, in despite of the rage and cruel mind of Jezebel. Daniel, with his companions, and Mordecai also, were exalted to earthly and temporal dignity, that they might in that state, they being men that abounded in the fear of God, be serviceable to their brethren in their straits and difficulties.

(9.) Another motive to grow in this grace of fear is: where the fear of God in the heart of any is not growing, there no grace thrives, nor duty done as it should be.

There no grace thrives; neither faith, hope, love, nor any grace. This is evident from that general exhortation; " Let us cleanse ourselves from all filthiness of the flesh and spirit, perfecting holiness in the fear of God," 2 Cor. vii. 1. Perfecting holiness; what is that? But as James says of patience, let every grace have its " perfect work, that ye may be perfect and entire, wanting nothing," James i. 4.

But this cannot be done but in the fear of God; yea, in the exercise of that grace, and so, consequently, in the growth of it; for there is no grace but grows, being exercised. If then you would be perfect in holiness, if you would have every grace that God has put into your souls grow and flourish unto perfection; lay them, as I may say, to soak in this grace of fear, and do all in the exercise of it; for a little done in the fear of the Lord, is better than the revenues of the wicked, Prov. xvi. 8. And again; the Lord will not suffer the soul of the righteous, the soul that liveth in the fear of the Lord, to famish; but he casteth away the abundance of the wicked.   Bring abundance to God, and if it be not seasoned with godly fear, it shall not be accept- able to him, but loathsome and abominable in his sight; for it doth not flow from the spirit of the fear of the Lord.

Therefore, where there is not a growth in this fear, there is no duty done acceptably.   This flows from that which goes before, for if grace rather de- cays than grows, where this grace of fear is not in the growth and increase thereof, then duties in their glory and acceptableness decay likewise.

(10.) Another motive to stir thee up to grow in the increase of this grace of fear, is: it is a grace, that if you abound therein, will give you great boldness both with God and men.   Job was a man, a nonsuch in his day, for one that feared God; and who so bold with God as Job?   Who so bold with God, and who so bold with men as he?

How bold was he with God, when he wished for nothing more than that he might come even to his seat; and concluded, that if he could come at him, he would approach even as a prince unto him, and as such would order his cause before him!

Also, before his friends, how bold was he! for ever as they laid to his charge that he was an hypo- crite, he repels them with the testimony of a good conscience; which good conscience he got, and kept, and maintained, by increasing in the fear of God; yea, his conscience was kept so good by this grace of fear, (for it was by that he eschewed evil,) that it was common with him to appeal to God when accused, and also to put himself, for his clearing, under most bitter curses and imprecations.

This fear of God is it that keeps the conscience clean and tender, and so free from much of that defilement that even a good man may be afflicted with, for want of this growth in the fear of God.

Yea, let me add, if a man can, with a good conscience, say, that he desires to fear the name of God, it will add boldness to his soul in his approaches into the presence of God. "O Lord," said Nehemiah, "I beseech thee, let now thine ear be attentive to the prayer of thy servants, who desire to fear thy name," Neh. i. 11.

He pleaded his desire of fearing the name of God as an argument with God to grant him his request; and the reason was, because God had promised before to bless them that fear him, both small and great.

(11.) Another motive to stir you up to fear the Lord, and to grow in this fear, is: by it thou mayest have thy labours blessed to the saving of the souls of others. It is said of Levi, (of whom mention was made before that he feared God, and was afraid before his name,) that he saved others from their sins. "The law of truth was in his mouth, and iniquity was not found in his lips: and he walked with me in peace and equity, and did turn many away from iniquity," Mal. ii. 6. The fear of God that dwelt in his heart, showed its growth in the sanctifying of the Lord by his life and words; and the Lord also blessed this his growth herein, by blessing his labours to the saving of his neighbours.

Wouldst thou save thy husband, thy wife, thy children? then be greatly in the fear of God. This Peter teaches: "Wives, be in subjection to your own husbands; that, if any obey not the word, they also may without the word be won

by the conversation of the wives; while they behold your chaste conversation coupled with fear,"
1 Pet. iii. 1, 2.

So, then, if wives and children, yea, if husbands,
wives, children, servants, etc., did but better observe this general rule of Peter, namely, of letting
their whole conversation be coupled with fear,
they might be made instruments in God's hand of
much more good than they are. But the misery is,
the fear of God is wanting in actions, and that is the
cause that so little good is done by those that pro-
fess. It is not a conversation that is coupled with a
profession, for a great profession may be attended
with a life that is not good, but scandalous; but it is
a conversation coupled with fear of God, that is, with
the impressions of the fear of God upon it; which
is convincing, and which ministereth the awakenings
of God to the conscience, in order to saving the unbeliever. Oh, they are a sweet couple, namely, a
Christian conversation coupled with fear.

The want of this fear of God is that which oftentimes has been a stumbling block to the blind.
Alas, the world will not be convinced by your talk,
by your notions, and by the great profession that
you make, if they see not therewith mixed the lively
impressions of the fear of God; but will, as I said,
rather stumble and fall, even at your conversation,
and at your profession itself. Wherefore, to prevent
this mischief, that is, of stumbling of souls while you
make your profession of God, by a conversation not
becoming your profession, God bids you fear him;
implying, that a good conversation, coupled with
fear, delivers the blind world from those falls that
otherwise they cannot be delivered from. "Thou
shalt not curse the deaf, nor put a stumbling-block

before the blind, but shalt fear thy God : I am the
Lord," Levit. xix. 14.

"But shalt fear thy God." That is the remedy that
will prevent their stumbling at you, at what else soever they stumble. Wherefore Paul says to Timothy,
"Take heed unto thyself, and unto the doctrine ;
continue in them : for in doing this thou shalt both
save thyself, and them that hear thee," 1 Tim. iv. 16.

(12.) Another motive to fear, and to grow in this
fear of God, is : this is the way to engage God to deliver thee from many outward dangers, whoever falls
therein.

This is proved from the history of the Hebrew
midwives. "The midwives," says Moses, " feared
God, and did not drown the men-children, as the
king had commanded, but saved them alive." And
what follows? "Therefore God dealt well with
the midwives: and the people multiplied, and
waxed very mighty. And it came to pass, because
the midwives feared God, that he made them
houses," Exod. i. 17, 20, 21 ; that is, he sheltered
them, and caused them to be hid from the rage and
fury of the king, and that perhaps in some of the
houses of the Egyptians themselves ; for why might
not the midwives be there hid as well as was Moses,
even in the king's court ?

And how many times are those that fear God said
to be delivered, both by God and his holy angels, as
I have already shown.

(13.) Another motive to fear, and to grow in this
fear of God, is : this is the way to be delivered from
errors and damnable opinions. There are some that
perish in their righteousness ; that is an error. There
are some that perish in their wickedness ; and that is
an error also. Some, again, prolong their lives by

o

their wickedness, and others are righteous over much ; and also some are over wise : and all these are snares, and pits, and holes. But then, sayest thou, how shall I escape? Indeed, that is the question, and the Holy Ghost resolves it thus : " He that feareth God shall come forth of them all," Eccles. vii. 18.

(14.) Another motive to fear, and to grow in this fear of God, is : such have leave, be they never so dark in their souls, to come boldly to Jesus Christ, and to trust in him for life. I told you before, that those that fear God have, in the general, a licence to trust in him ; but now I tell you, and that in particular, that they, and they especially, may do it, and that though in the dark. You that sit in darkness, and have no light, if this grace of fear be alive in your hearts, you have this boldness : " Who is among you that feareth the Lord, that obeyeth the voice of his servant, that walketh in darkness, and hath no light? let him trust in the name of the Lord, and stay upon his God," Isa. l. 10.

It is no small advantage, you know, when men have to deal in difficult matters, to have a patent or licence to deal :· now, to trust in the Lord is a difficult thing, yet the best and most gainful of all. But then, some will say, since it is so difficult, how may we do without danger? Why the text gives a licence, a patent to those to trust in his name that have his fear in their hearts. " Let him trust in the name of the Lord, and stay upon his God."

(15.) Another motive to fear, and to grow in the grace of fear, is : God will own and acknowledge such to be his, whoever he rejecteth. Yea, he will distinguish and separate them from all others in the day of his terrible judgments.

He will do with them as he did by those that sighed for the abominations that were done in the land, command the man that hath his inkhorn by his side to set a mark upon their foreheads, that they might not fall in that judgment with others.

So God says plainly of those that feared the Lord, and that thought upon his name, that they should be written in his book: "A book of remembrance was written before him for them that feared the Lord, and that thought upon his name. And they shall be mine, saith the Lord of hosts, in that day when I make up my jewels; and I will spare them, as a man spareth his own son that serveth him," Mal. iii. 16, 17.

Mark; he both acknowledges them for his, and also promises to spare them as a man would spare his own son. Yea, moreover, he will wrap them up as his chief jewels in the bundle of' life. Thus much for the motives.

Having given you these motives to the duty of growing in this fear of God, before I leave this use, I will, in few words, show you how you may grow in this fear of God.

1. First, then, if thou wouldst grow in this fear of God, learn aright to distinguish of fear in general. I mean, learn to distinguish between that fear that is godly, and that which in itself is indeed ungodly fear of God, and know them well the one from the other, lest the one, the fear that in itself indeed is ungodly, get the place, even the upper hand, of that which truly is godly fear. And remember the ungodly fear of God, is by God himself counted an enemy to him, and hurtful to his people, and is therefore most plentifully forbidden in the word.

2. If thou wouldst grow in this godly fear,

learn rightly to distinguish it from that fear in
particular that is godly but for a time; even from
that fear that is wrought from the Spirit, as a Spirit
of bondage. I say, learn to distinguish this from
that, and also perfectly to know the bounds that God
hath set to that fear that is wrought by the Spirit,
as a Spirit of bondage; lest, instead of growing in
the fear that is to abide with thy soul for ever, thou
be overrun again with that first fear, which is to
abide with thee but till the Spirit of adoption come.
And that you may not only distinguish them one
from the other, but also keep each in its due place
and bounds, consider, in general, of what hath already
been said upon this head, and, in particular, that the
first fear is no more wrought by the Holy Spirit,
but by the devil, to distress thee, and make thee to
live, not like a son, but a slave. And for thy better
help in this matter, know that God himself hath set
bounds to this fear, and has concluded that after the
Spirit of adoption is come, that other fear is wrought
in thy heart by him no more.

Again; before I leave this, let me tell thee, that if
thou dost not well bestir thee in this matter, this
bondage fear, namely, that which is like it, though
not wrought in thee by the Holy Ghost, will, by the
management and subtilty of the devil, the author of
it, haunt, disturb, and make thee live uncomfortably,
and that while thou art an heir of God and his
kingdom. This is that fear that the apostle speaks
of, that makes men all their lifetime subject to
bondage, Heb. ii. 15.

For though Christ will deliver thee indeed at last,
thou having embraced him by faith, yet thy life will
be full of trouble; and death, though Jesus hath
abolished it, will be always a frightful object to thee,

in all thy ways and thoughts, to break thy peace, and to make thee to draw thy loins heavily after him.

3. Wouldst thou grow in this godly fear ? Then as thou shouldst learn to distinguish of fears, so thou shouldst make conscience of which to entertain and cherish. If God would have his fear, (and it is called his fear by way of eminency; "That his fear may be before you, that you sin not," Exod. xx. 20;) I say, if God would have this his fear be with thee, then thou shouldst make conscience of this, and not so lightly give way to slavish fear as is common for Christians to do.

There is utterly a fault among Christians about this thing; that is, they make not that conscience of resisting slavish fear as they ought; they rather cherish and entertain it, and so weaken themselves and that fear which they ought to strengthen. And this is the reason that we so often lie struggling under the black and amazing thoughts that are engendered in our hearts by unbelief: for this fear nourisheth unbelief; that is, now it doth, namely, if we give way to it after the Spirit of adoption is come, and readily closeth with all the fiery darts of the wicked.

But Christians are ready to do with this fear as the horse does when the spur is set against his side, even lean to it until it entereth into his belly. We lean naturally to this fear, I mean, after God has done good to our souls: it is hard striving against it, because it has even our sense and feeling on its side.

But I say, if thou wouldst be a growing Christian, growing, I say, in the fear that is godly, in the fear that is always so; then make conscience of striving against the other, and against all these things that would bring thee back to it. Wherefore

o 3

should I fear," said David, " in the days of evil,
when the iniquity of my heels shall compass me
about ?" Psa. xlix. 5.

What! not fear in the day of evil? What! not
when the iniquity of thy heels compasseth thee
about? No, not then, says he; that is, not with
that fear that would bring him again into bondage
to the law; for he had received the Spirit of adoption before. Indeed, if ever a Christian has ground
to give way to slavish fear, it is at these two times,
namely, in the day of evil, and when the iniquity of
his heels compasseth him about. But you see
David would not then, no, not then, give way
thereto; nor did he see reason why he should.
" Wherefore should I ?" said he. Wherefore, indeed! since now thou art become a son of God
through Christ, and hast received the Spirit of his
Son into thy heart, crying, Father, Father.

4. Wouldst thou grow in this grace of godly
fear? then grow in the knowledge of the new
covenant; for that is indeed the girdle of our
reins, and the strength of our souls. Hear what
Zacharias saith, " God hath raised up an horn of
salvation for us in the house of his servant David;
as he spake by the mouth of his holy prophets,
which have been since the world began," Luke i.
69, 70. But what was it that he spake? Why,
" That he would grant unto us, that we being delivered out of the hand of our enemies might serve
him without fear, in holiness and righteousness before him all the days of our life," ver. 74, 75. But
upon what is this princely, fearless, service of God
grounded? Why, upon the holy covenant of God,
upon the oath that he swore unto Abraham.

Now, in this covenant is wrapped up all thy salvation; in it is contained all thy desire; and I am sure that then it containeth the complete salvation of thy soul; and, I say, since this covenant is confirmed by promise, by oath, and by the blood of the Son of God, and that on purpose that thou mightest serve thy God without slavish fear, then the knowledge and faith of this covenant are of absolute necessity to bring us into this liberty, and out of our slavish terrors, and so, consequently, to cause us to grow in that sonlike, godly fear, which became even the Son of God himself, and becomes all his disciples to live in the growth and exercise of.

5. Wouldst thou grow in this godly fear? then labour even always to keep thine evidences for heaven and of thy salvation alive upon thy heart; for he that loseth his evidences for heaven will hardly keep slavish fear out of his heart; but he that hath the wisdom and grace to keep them alive, and apparent to himself, will grow in this godly fear. See how David words it : " From the end of the earth will I cry unto thee, when my heart is overwhelmed : lead me to the rock that is higher than I. For thou hast been a shelter for me, and a strong tower from the enemy. I will abide in thy tabernacle for ever : I will trust in the covert of thy wings. For thou, O God, hast heard my vows : thou hast given me the heritage of those that fear thy name," Psa. lxi. 2—5.

Mark a little. David doth, by these words, in the first place, suggest, that sometimes, to his thinking, he was as far off from his God as the ends of the earth are asunder, and that at such times he was subject to be overwhelmed, or afraid. Secondly, the way that he took at such times to help himself was, to cry to God to lead him again to Jesus

Christ; "Lead me to the Rock that is higher than I." For, indeed, without faith in him, and the renewing of that faith, there can be no evidence for heaven made to appear unto the soul. This, therefore, he prays for first. Then he puts that faith into exercise, and that with respect to the time that was past, and also of the time that was to come. For the time past, says he, "Thou hast been a shelter to me, and a strong tower from the enemy;" and for the time to come he said, "I will abide in thy tabernacle;" that is, in thy Christ by faith, and in thy way of worship by love, for ever. And observe, he makes the believing remembrance of his first evidences for heaven the ground of this his cry and faith; "For thou," says he, "O God, hast given me the heritage of those that fear thy name." Thou hast made me meet to be partaker of the mercy of thy chosen, and hast put me under the blessing of goodness wherewith thou hast blessed those that fear thee.

Thus you see how David, in his distresses, musters up his prayers, faith, and evidences for eternal life, that he might deliver himself from being overwhelmed, that is, with slavish fear, and that he might also abound in that sonlike fear of his fellow-brethren, which is not only comely with respect to our profession, but profitable to our souls.

6. Wouldst thou grow in this fear of God? then set before thine eyes the being and majesty of God; for that both begetteth, maintaineth, and increaseth this fear; and hence it is called the fear of God, that is, an holy and awful dread and reverence of his majesty: for the fear of God is to stand in awe of him, but how can that be done if we do not set him before us? And again; if we would fear

him more, we must abide more in the sense and
faith of his glorious majesty.   Hence this fear and
God's name are so often put together : as, Fear God;
Fear the Lord;   Fear thy God;   Do this in the fear of
the Lord; and, Thou shalt fear thy God, I am the Lord.

For these words, "I am the Lord thy God," and
the like, are on purpose put in, not only to show us
whom we should fear, but also to beget, maintain,
and increase in us that fear that is due from us to
that glorious and fearful name, the Lord our God.

7. Wouldst thou grow in this grace of fear ?
then keep always close to thy conscience the
authority of the word; fear the commandment,
as the commandment of a God both mighty and
glorious, and as the commandment of a Father, both
loving and pitiful.   Let this commandment, I say,
be always with thine eye, with thine ear, and with
thine heart; for then thou wilt be taught, not only
to fear, but to abound in the fear of the Lord.
Every grace is nourished by the word, and without
it there is no thrift in the soul.

8. Wouldst thou grow in this grace of fear ?
then be much in the faith of the promise, of the
promise that maketh over to thy soul an interest in
God, by Christ, and of all good things.   The promise
naturally tendeth to increase in us the fear of the
Lord, because this fear grows by goodness and mercy.
"They shall fear the Lord and his goodness,"
Hos. iii. 5.   Now, this goodness and mercy of God is
wrapped up in, and made over to us by promise;   for
God gave it to Abraham by promise.   Therefore,
the faith and hope of the promise causeth this fear to
grow in the soul.   "Having therefore these promises,
dearly beloved, let us cleanse ourselves from all
filthiness of the flesh and spirit, perfecting holiness

in the fear of God," 2 Cor. vii. 1.   Perfect holiness
in the fear of God; therefore that fear by the promise must needs grow mighty, for by, with, and in
it, you see, holiness is perfected.

9. Wouldst thou grow in this grace of fear?
then remember the judgments of God that have
or shall certainly overtake those professors that
have either been downright hypocrites, or else un-
watchful Christians ; for both these sorts partake of
the judgments of God : the one, namely, the true
Christian, for his unwatchfulness, for his correction ;
the other, namely, the hypocrite, for his hypocrisy, to
his destruction.   This is the way to make thee stand
in awe, and to make thee tremble, and grow in the
grace of fear before thy God.

Judgments! you may say; what judgments?

Ans. Time would fail me here to tell thee of the
judgments that sometimes overtake God's people,
and that always certainly overtake the hypocrite for
his transgressions.

For those that attend God's people, I would have
thee look back to the place in this book where they
are particularly touched upon.

And for those that attend the hypocrite, in general
they are these :—Blindness of heart in this world ;
the death of their hope at the day of their death ;
and the damnation of their souls at the day of
judgment.

The godly consideration of these things tend to
make men grow in the fear of God.

10. Wouldst thou grow in this grace of fear?
then study the excellences of the grace of fear,
and what profit it yieldeth to those that have it ;
and labour to get thy heart into the love, both of the
exercise of the grace itself, and also of the fruit it

yieldeth; for a man hardly grows in the increase of any grace until his heart is united to it, and until it is made lovely in his eyes.

Now, the excellences of this grace of fear have also been discoursed of in this book before, where, by reading, thou shalt find the fruit it bears, and the promises that are annexed to it, which, because they are many, I refer thee also thither for thy instruction.

11. Wouldst thou grow in this grace of fear? then remember what a world of privileges do belong to those that fear the Lord, as also I have hinted; namely, that such shall not be hurt, shall want no good thing, shall be guarded by angels, and have a special licence, though in ever so dreadful plight, to trust in the name of the Lord, and stay upon their God.

12. Wouldst thou grow in this grace of fear? then be much in prayer to God for abundance of the increase thereof. To fear God is that which is according to his will; and "if we ask any thing according to his will, he heareth us," 1 John v. 14. Pray, therefore, that God would unite thy heart to fear his name; this is the way to grow in the grace of fear.

13. Wouldst thou grow in this grace of fear? then devote thyself to it. Devote myself to it, you will say; how is that? I answer, Why give thyself to it; addict thyself to it; solace thyself in the contemplation of God, and of a reverence of his name, and word, and worship; then wilt thou fear, and grow in this grace of fear.

And that I may yet be helpful to thee, I shall now give thee caution of those things that will, if way be given to them, hinder thy growth in this fear of God, the which, because they are very hurtful to the people of God, I would have thee be warned by them.

And they are these which follow :—·

(1.) If thou wouldst grow in this grace of fear, take heed of an hard heart; for that will hinder thy growth in this grace. "Why hast thou made us to err from thy ways, and hardened our heart from thy fear?" Isa. lxiii. 17, was a bitter complaint of the church heretofore; for it is not only the judgment that in itself is dreadful and sore to God's people, but that which greatly hindereth the growth of this grace in the soul. A hard heart is but barren ground for any grace to grow in, especially for the grace of fear; there is but little of this fear where the heart indeed is hard, neither will there ever be much therein.

Now, if thou wouldst be kept from a hard heart, take heed of the beginnings of sin. Take heed, I say, of that, though it should be ever so small. "A little leaven leavens the whole lump," 1 Cor. v. 6. There is more in a little sin to harden than in a great deal of grace to soften. David's look upon Bathsheba was, one would think, but a small matter; yet that beginning of sin contracted such hardness of heart in him, that it carried him almost beyond all fear of God. It carried him to commit lewdness with her, murder upon the body of Uriah, and to abundance of wicked dissimulation; which are things, I say, that have direct tendency to quench and destroy all fear of God in the soul.

If thou hast sinned, lie not down without repentance; for the want of repentance, after one has sinned, makes the heart yet harder and harder.

Indeed, a hard heart is impenitent, and impenitence also makes the heart harder and harder.

THE FEAR OF GOD.

So that if impenitence be added to hardness of heart, or to the beginnings of sin, which makes it so, it will quickly be with that soul as is said of the house of Israel, "Thou refusedst to be ashamed," Jer. iii. 3.

If thou wouldst be rid of a hard heart, that great enemy to the growth of the grace of fear, be much with Christ upon the cross in thy meditations, for that is an excellent remedy against hardness of heart; a right sight of him, as he hanged there for thy sins, will dissolve thy heart into tears, and make it soft and tender. "They shall look upon me whom they have pierced, and they shall mourn," Zech. xii. 10. Now, a soft, a tender, and broken heart is a fit place for the grace of fear to thrive in.

(2.) If thou wouldst have the grace of fear to grow in thy soul, take heed also of a prayerless heart, for that is not a place for this grace of fear to grow in. Hence, he that refraineth prayer is said to cast off fear. "Thou castest off fear," said one of his friends to Job. But how did he do that? Why, the next words show: "Thou restrainest prayer before God," Job xv. 4. Seest thou a professor that prayeth not? That man thrusteth the fear of God away from him. Seest thou a man that prays but little? That man feareth God but little; for it is the praying soul, the man that is mighty in praying, that has an heart for the fear of God to grow in. Take heed, therefore, of a prayerless heart, if thou wouldst grow in this grace of the fear of God.

Prayer is as the pitcher that fetcheth water from the brook, therewith to water the herbs; break the pitcher, and it will fetch no water, and for want of water the garden withers.

(3.) Wouldst thou grow in this grace of fear? then

P

take heed of a light and wanton heart; for neither is such a heart good ground for the fear of God to grow in. Wherefore it is said of Judah, that she "feared not, but went and played the harlot also," Jer. iii. 8. She was given to wantonness, and to be light, and vain, and so her fear of God decayed. Had Joseph been as wanton as his mistress, he had been as void of the fear of God as she; but he was of a sober, tender, godly, considerate spirit, therefore he grew in the fear of God.

(4.) Wouldst thou grow in this grace of fear? then take heed of a covetous heart; for neither is that good ground for this grace of fear to grow in. Therefore, this covetousness and the fear of God are as enemies, set the one in opposition to the other: "Such as fear God, men of truth, hating covetousness," Exod. xviii. 21.

And the reason why covetousness is such an obstruction to the growth of this grace of fear, is because covetousness casteth those things out of the heart which alone can nourish this fear. It casteth out the word and love of God, without which no grace can grow in the soul. How then should the fear of God grow in a covetous heart?

(5.) Wouldst thou grow in this grace of fear? then take heed of an unbelieving heart; for an unbelieving heart is not good ground for this grace of fear to grow in. An unbelieving heart is called "an evil heart," Heb. iii. 12, because from it flows all the wickedness that is committed in the world. Now, it is faith, or a believing heart, that nourisheth this fear of God, and not the other; and the reason is, for that faith brings God, heaven, and hell to the soul, and maketh it duly consider them all. This is, therefore, the means of fear, and that which will make it grow in the soul; but unbelief is a bane thereto.

(6.) Wouldst thou grow in this grace of fear? Then take heed of a forgetful heart. Such a heart is not a heart where the grace of fear will flourish. "When I remember I am afraid, and trembling taketh hold on my flesh," Job xxi. 6. Therefore take heed of forgetfulness; do not forget, but remember God, and his kindness, patience, and mercy to those that yet neither have grace nor special favour from him, and that will beget and nourish his fear in 'thy heart; but forgetfulness of this, or of any other of his judgments, is a great wound and weakening to this fear. When a man well remembers that God's judgments are so great a deep and mystery, as indeed they are, that remembrance puts a man upon such considerations of God and of his judgments as to make him fear. Therefore, says Job, I am afraid of him: "Therefore am I troubled at his presence: when I consider, I am afraid of him," Job xxiii. 15: when I remember and consider of the wonderful depths of his judgments toward man.

(7.) Wouldst thou grow in this grace of fear? then take heed of a murmuring and repining heart; for that is not a heart for this grace of fear to grow in.

As, for instance, when men murmur and repine at God's hand, at his dispensations, and at the judgments that overtake them, in their persons, estates, families, or relations, that their murmuring tendeth to destroy fear; for a murmuring spirit is such an one as seems to correct God, and to find fault with his dispensations; and where there is that, the heart is far from fear.

A murmuring spirit either comes from that wisdom

that pretends to understand that there is a failure
in the nature and execution of things, or from
an envy and spite at the execution of them. Now, if
murmurings arise from this pretended wisdom of the
flesh, then, instead of fearing God, his actions are
judged to be either rigid or ridiculous, which yet are
done in judgment, truth, and righteousness. So that
a murmuring heart cannot be a good one for the fear
of God to grow in; alas! the heart where that
grows must be a soft one, as Job says, "God maketh
my heart soft," Job xxiii. 16; and a heart that will
stoop, and be silent at the most abstruse of all his
judgments: "I was dumb, I opened not my mouth;
because thou didst it," Psa. xxxix. 9.

The heart in which this fear of God doth flourish,
is such, that it bows, and is mute, if it can but espy
the hand, wisdom, justice, or holiness of God in this
or the other of his dispensations, and so stirs up the
soul to fear before him. But if this murmuring
ariseth from envy and spite, that looketh so like to
the spirit of the devil, that nothing need be said
to give conviction of the horrible wickedness of it.

(8.) Wouldst thou grow in this grace of fear? then
take heed of a high and captious spirit; for that is
not good ground for the fear of God to grow in: a
meek and quiet spirit is the best, and there the fear
of God will flourish most; therefore, Peter puts
meekness and fear together, as being most suited in
their nature and natural tendency one to another,
1 Peter iii. 15.

Meekness of spirit is like that ground that hath
depth of earth in it, in which things may take root
and grow; but an high and captious spirit is like to
the stony ground, where there is not depth of earth,
and consequently where this grace of fear cannot

grow.   Therefore, take heed of this kind of spirit, if thou wouldst that the fear of God should grow in thy soul.

(9.) Wouldst thou grow in the grace of fear? then take heed of an envious heart; for that is not a good heart for the fear of God to grow in.   "Let not thine heart envy sinners: but be thou in the fear of the Lord all the day long," Prov. xxiii. 17.   To envy any is a sign of a bad spirit; and that man takes upon him, as I have already hinted, to be a controller and a judge, yea, and a malicious executioner too, and that of the fury that ariseth from his own lusts and revengeful spirit, upon, perhaps, the man that is more righteous than himself.   But suppose he is a sinner that is the object of thine envy, why the text sets that envy in direct opposition to the fear of God: " Envy not sinners, but be thou in the fear of the Lord." These two, therefore, namely, envy to sinners and fearing of God, are opposites. Thou canst not fear God and envy sinners too.   And the reason is, because he that envieth a sinner hath forgotten himself that he is as bad, and how can he then fear God?   He that envies sinners rejects his duty of blessing of those that curse, and praying for those that despitefully use us; and how can he that hath rejected this fear God?   He that envieth sinners, therefore, cannot be of a good spirit, nor can the fear of God grow in his heart.

(10.) Wouldst thou grow in this grace of fear? then take heed of hardening thy heart at any time against convictions to particular duties, as to prayer, alms, self-denial, or the like.   Take heed, also, of hardening thy heart when thou art under any judgments of God, as sickness, losses, crosses, or the like.

I bade you before to beware of a hard heart; but

now I bid you beware of hardening your soft ones ; for to harden the heart is to make it worse than it is, harder, more desperate, and bold against God than at the present it is. Now, I say, if thou wouldst grow in this grace of fear, take heed of hardening thy heart, and especially of hardening it against convictions to good; for those convictions are sent of God, like seasonable showers of rain, to keep the tillage of thy heart in good order, that the grace of fear may grow therein ; but this stifling of convictions makes the heart as hard as a piece of the nether millstone.

Therefore, happy is he that receiveth conviction, for so he doth keep in the fear of God, and that fear is thereby nourished in his soul; but cursed is he that doth otherwise. " Happy is the man that feareth alway : but he that hardeneth his heart shall fall into mischief," Prov. xxviii. 14.

III. I come now to a use of encouragement to those that are blessed with this grace of fear. The last text that was mentioned saith, " Happy is the man that feareth alway," and so doth many more. Happy already, because blessed with this grace ; and happy for time to come, because this grace shall abide and continue till the soul that hath it is brought unto the mansion-house of glory. " I will put my fear in their hearts, that they shall not depart from me," Jer. xxxii. 40. Therefore, as here it saith, " Happy is he," so it saith also, " It shall be well with them," that is, in time to come : " It shall be well with them that fear God," Eccles. viii. 12. Had God given thee all the world, yet cursed hadst thou been, if he had not given thee the fear of the Lord ; for the fashion of this world is a fading thing, but he that feareth the Lord shall abide for ever and ever.

This, therefore, is the first thing that I would propound for thy encouragement, O thou man that fearest the Lord.

This grace will dwell in thy heart, for it is a new covenant grace, and will abide with thee for ever. It is sent to thee from God, not only to join thy heart unto him, but to keep thee from final apostasy: " I will put my fear in their hearts, that they shall not depart from me," Jer. xxxii. 40. That thou mayst never forsake God is his design, therefore to keep thee from that wicked thing he hath put his fear in thy heart.

Many are the temptations, difficulties, snares, traps, trials, and troubles, that the people of God pass through in the world; but how shall they be kept, how shall they be delivered, and escape? Why, the answer is, the fear of God will keep them; " He that feareth God shall come forth of them all," Eccl. vii. 18.

Is it not, therefore, a wonderful mercy to be blessed with this grace of fear, that thou by it mayst be kept from final, which is damnable, apostasy? Bless God, therefore, thou blessed man, that hast this grace of fear in thy soul.

There are five things in this grace of fear that have a direct tendency in them to keep thee from final apostasy.

1. It is seated in the heart; and the heart is, as I may call it, the main fort in the mystical world, man. It is not placed in the head, as knowledge is; nor in the mouth, as utterance is; but in the heart, the seat of all. " I will put my fear in their heart." If a king would keep a town secure to himself, let him be sure to man sufficiently the main fort thereof. If he have twenty thousand men well armed, if they lie scattered here and there, the town may be taken

for all that; but if the main fort be well manned, then the town is more secure. What if a man had all the parts, yea, all the arts of men and angels, they would not keep the heart to God. But when the heart, this principal fort, is possessed with the fear of God, then he is safe, but not else.

2. As the heart in general, so the will in special, that chief and great faculty of the soul, is the principle that is actuated by this fear.

The will, which way that goes, all goes; if it be to heaven or hell. Now, the will, I say, is that main faculty that is governed by this fear that doth possess the soul, therefore, all is likely to go well with it.

This Samuel teacheth, where he saith, "If ye will fear the Lord," 1 Sam. xii. 14. Fearing God is a voluntary act of the will, and that being so, the soul is kept from rebellion against the commandment, because by the will, where this fear of God is placed, and which it governeth, is led all the rest of the powers of the soul. In this will, then, is the fear of God placed, that this grace may the better be able to govern the soul, and so, by consequence, the whole man; for, as I said before, look what way the will goes, look what the will does, thither goes, and that does the whole man.

Man, when his will is alienated from God, is reckoned rebellious throughout, and that not without ground, for the will is the principal faculty of the soul as to obedience, and therefore things done without the will are as if they were not done at all. "The spirit is willing;" "If ye be willing;" "She hath done what she could," and the like; by these and such like sayings, the goodness of the heart and action is judged, as to the subjective part thereof.

Now, this fear that we have been speaking of, is

placed in the soul, and so, consequently, in the will, that the man may thereby the better be kept from final and damnable apostasy.

3. This fear, as I may say, even above every other grace, is God's well-wisher; and hence it is called, as I also have shown you, his fear. As he also says, in the text mentioned before, " I will put my fear in their hearts." These words " his " and " my " are intimate and familiar expressions, bespeaking not only great favour to man, but a very great trust put in him. As if he should say, This fear is my special friend, it will subject and bow the soul, and the several faculties thereof, to my pleasure; it is my great favourite, and subdueth sinners to my pleasure. You shall rarely find faith, or repentance, or parts, go under such familiar characters as this blessed fear of the Lord doth. Of all the counsellors and mighties that David had, Hushi only was called the king's friend: so of all the graces of the Spirit, this of the fear of God goes mostly, if not always, by the title of " my fear," " God's fear," " his fear," etc.

I told you before, if the king will keep a town, the main fort therein must be sufficiently manned; and now I will add, that if he have not to govern those men some trusty and special friend, such as Hushi was to David, he may find it lost when it should stand him in greatest stead. If a soul should be possessed with all things possible, yet if this fear of God be wanting, all other things will give place in time of rebellion, and the soul shall be found in, and under the conduct of hell, when it should stand up for God and his truth in the world. This fear of God is God's special friend, and, therefore, it has given unto it the chief seat of the heart, the will, that

the whole man may now be, and also be kept hereafter, in the subjection and obedience of the gospel.

4. This grace of fear is the softest and most tender of God's honour of any other grace. It is that
tender, sensible, and trembling grace that keeps
the soul upon its continual watch. To keep a good
watch is, you know, a wonderful safety to a place
that is in continual danger because of the enemy.
This is the grace that setteth the watch, and that
keepeth the watchman awake.

A man cannot watch as he should, if he be destitute of fear ; let him be confident, and he sleeps, he
unadvisedly lets into the garrison those that should
not come there. Israel's fault, when they came to
Canaan, was, that they made a covenant with the
inhabitants of the land, namely, the Gibeonites, without asking counsel of God. But would they have
done so, think you, if, at the same time, the fear of
God had had its full play in the soul, in the army ?
No ; they at that time forgot to fear. The grace of
fear had not, at that time, its full stroke and sway
among them.

5. This grace of fear is that which, as I may so
say, first affects the hearts of saints with judgments,
after we have sinned, and so is a beginning grace to
bring again that to rights that by sin is put out of
frame. Oh, it is a precious grace of God. I know
what I say in this matter, and also where I had been
long ago, through the power of my lusts, and the
wiles of the devil, had it not been for the fear
of God.

But, secondly, another encouragement for those
that are blessed with this blessed grace of fear is
this : this fear fails not to do this work for the soul,
if there in truth, be it ever so small in measure. A

little of this leaven leavens the whole lump. True, a little will not do, or help the soul to do those worthy exploits in the heart or life, as well as a bigger measure thereof; nor indeed can a little of any grace do that which a bigger measure will; but a little will preserve the soul from final apostasy, and deliver it into the arms of the Son of God at the final judgment. Wherefore, when he saith, " I will put my fear in their heart," he says not, I will put so much of it there, such a quantity, or such a degree, but, " I will put my fear there."

I speak not this in the least to tempt the godly man to be content with the least degree of the fear of God in his heart. True, men should be glad that God hath put even the least degree of this grace into their souls; but they should not be content therewith; they should earnestly covet more, pray for more, and use all lawful, that is, all the means of God's appointing, that they may get more.

There are, as I have said, several degrees of this grace of fear, and our wisdom is, to grow in it, as in all other graces of the Spirit. The reasons why I have already shown you, and also the way to grow therein; but the least measure thereof will keep the soul from final apostasy. There are, as I have shown you, those that greatly fear the Lord, that fear exceedingly, and that fear him above many of their brethren; but the small in this grace are saved, as well as those that are great therein: "He will reward them that fear him, small and great," Rev. xi. 18.

This fear of the Lord is the pulse of the soul, and as some pulses beat stronger, some weaker, so is this grace of fear in the soul. Those that beat best are a sign of best life, but those that beat worst show that

life is present : as long as the pulse beats we count
not that the man is dead, though weak ; and this
fear, where it is, preserves to everlasting life. Pulses
there are, also, that are intermitting, namely, such as
have their times for a little ; a little time to stop, and
then beat again. True, these are dangerous pulses,
but yet a sign of life. This fear of God, also, is sometimes like this intermitting pulse ; there are times
when it forbears to work, and then it works again.
David had an intermitting pulse ; Peter had an intermitting pulse ; as also many other of the saints of
God. I call that an intermitting pulse, with reference to the fear we speak of, when there is some obstruction by the workings of corruptions in the soul ;
I say some obstruction from and hindrance of the
continual motion of this fear of God, yet none of
these, though they are various, and some of them
signs of weakness, are signs of death, but life. " I
will put my fear in their hearts, that they shall not
depart from me," Jer. xxxii. 40.

But you may say, How shall I know that I fear
God ?

Ans. If I should say that desires, true sincere
desires to fear him, is fear itself, I should not say
amiss ; for although a desire to be or do so and so
makes not a man to be, in temporal or natural things,
what he desires to be ; for a sick, or poor, or impri-
soned man may desire to be well, to be rich, or to
be at liberty, and yet be as they are, sick, poor, or
in prison : yet, in spirituals, a man's desire to be
good, to believe, to love, to hope, and fear God, doth
flow from the nature of grace itself.

I said before, that in temporals a man could not
properly be said to be what he was not ; yet a
man, even in naturals or temporals, shows his love to

that thing that he desires, whether it be health, riches, or liberty; and in spirituals, sincere desires, from love to this or that grace of God, flow from the root of the grace itself. "Thy servants, who desire to fear thy name," Neh. i. 11. Nehemiah bore himself before God upon this, that he desired to fear his name.

And hence, again, it is said concerning true desires, "The desire of a man is his kindness," Prov. xix. 22; for a man shows his heart, his love, his affections, and his delights, in his desires; and since the grace of the fear of God is a grace so pleasant in the sight of God, and of so sanctifying a nature in the soul where it is, a true sincere desire to be blessed with that grace must needs flow from some being of this grace in the soul already.

True desires are lower than higher acts of grace, but God will not overlook desires: "But now they desire a better country, that is, an heavenly: wherefore God is not ashamed to be called their God: for he hath prepared for them a city," Heb. xi. 16. Mark! they desire a country, and they shall have a city. At this low place, namely, sincere desires, God will meet the soul, and will tell him that he hath accepted of his desires, that his desires are his kindness, and flow from grace itself; "He will fulfil the desire of them that fear him," Psa. cxlv. 19. Therefore, desires are not rejected of God; but they would be if they did not flow from a principle of grace already in the soul; therefore, sincere desires to fear God, flow from grace already in the soul.

Therefore, since thou fearest God, and it is evident, by thy desires, that thou dost do so, thou art happy now in this thy fear, and shalt be happy for ever hereafter in the enjoyment of that which God, in another world, hath laid up for those that fear him.

3. Another encouragement for those that have this grace of fear is this: this grace can make that man that, in many other things, is not capable of serving God, serve him better than those that have all without it. Poor Christian man, thou hast scarcely been able to do any thing for God all thy days, but only to fear the Lord. Thou art no preacher, and so canst not do him service that way; thou art no rich man, and so canst not do him service with outward substance; thou art no wise man, and so canst not do any thing that way: but here is thy mercy, thou fearest God. Though thou canst not preach, thou canst fear God; though thou hast no bread to feed, nor fleece to clothe the poor, thou canst fear God. Oh, how blessed is the man that feareth the Lord, because this duty of fearing of God is an act of the mind, and may be done by the man that is destitute of all things but that holy and blessed mind!

Blessed, therefore, is that man, for God hath not laid the comfort of his people in the doing external duties, nor the salvation of their souls, but in believing, loving, and fearing God. Neither hath he laid these things in actions done in their health, nor in the due management of their most excellent parts, but in the receiving of Christ, and fear of God; the which, Christian, thou mayst do, and do acceptably, even though thou shouldst lie bed-ridden all thy days; thou mayst also be sick and believe, be sick and love, be sick and fear God, and so be a blessed man.

And here the poor Christian hath something to answer those that reproach him for his ignoble pedigree, and shortness of the glory of the wisdom of the world. True, may that man say, I was taken out of the dunghill, I was born in a base and low estate; but I fear God. I have no worldly greatness, nor excellency of natural parts; but I fear God.

When Obadiah met with Elijah, he gave him no worldly and fantastical compliment, nor did he glory in his promotion by Ahab, the king of Israel; but gravely, and after a gracious manner, said, " I thy servant fear the Lord from my youth," 1 Kings xviii. 12. Also, when the mariners inquired of Jonah, saying, " What is thine occupation? and whence comest thou? what is thy country? and of what people art thou?" this was the answer he gave them, " I am an Hebrew, and I fear the Lord, the God of heaven, which hath made the sea and the dry land," Jonah i. 8, 9.

Indeed, this answer is the highest and most noble in the world, nor are there any, save a few, that in truth can thus express themselves, though other answers they have enough. Most can say, I have wisdom, or might, or riches, or friends, or health, or the like; these are common, and are greatly boasted in by most: but he is the man that feareth God, and he that can say, when they say to him, What art thou? " I thy servant fear the Lord;" he is the man of many, he is to be honoured of men; though this, namely, that he feareth the Lord, is all that he hath in this world. He hath the thing, the honour, the life, and glory which are lasting; his blessedness will abide when other men's will be buried in the dust, in shame, and contempt.

Hypocrites! my last word is to you. The hypocrite is one that would appear to be that in men's

Q 2

eyes that he is nothing of in God's. Thou hypocrite! thou wouldst be esteemed to be one that loves
and that fears God, but does not, I have this to say
to thee; thy condition is damnable, because thou art
an hypocrite, and seekest to deceive both God and
man with guises, masks, shows, pretences, and thy
formal, carnal, feigned subjection to the outside of
statutes, laws, and commandments; but within thou
art full of rottenness and all excess.

Hypocrite! thou mayst, by thy cunning shifts, be
veiled and hid from men; but thou art naked before
the eyes of God; and he knoweth that his fear is not
in thy heart.

Hypocrite! be admonished that there is no obedience accepted of God where the heart is destitute of
this grace of fear.   Keeping the commandments is
but one part of the duty of man, and Paul did that,
even while he was an hypocrite.   To "fear God,
and keep his commandments: for this is the whole
duty of man," Eccles. xii. 13.   But to "fear God"
the hypocrite cannot as an hypocrite do, and therefore, as such, cannot escape the damnation of hell.

Hypocrite! thou must fear God first, even before
thou dost offer to meddle with the commandments,
that is, as to the keeping of them.   Indeed, thou
shouldst read therein that thou mayst learn to fear
the Lord; but yet, to "fear God" goes before the
command to keep his commandments; and if thou
dost not fear God first, thou transgresseth instead of
keeping the commandments.

Hypocrite! this word, "Fear God," is that which
the hypocrite quite forgets, although it is that which
sanctifies the whole duty of man; for this is that,
and nothing without it, that can make a man sincere
in his obedience.   The hypocrite looks for applause

abroad, and forgets that he is condemned at home; and both these he does because he wanteth the fear of God.

Hypocrite! be admonished that none of the privileges that are spoken of in the former part of the book belong to thee, because thou art an hypocrite; and if thou hope, thy hope shall be cut off; and if thou lean upon thy house, both thou and it shall fall into hell-fire. Triumph then; thy triumph is but for a while. Joy then; but "the joy of the hypocrite is but for a moment," Job xx. 5.

Perhaps thou wilt not let go now what, as an hypocrite, thou hast got. "What is the hope of the hypocrite, though he hath gained, when God taketh away his soul?" Job xxvii. 8.

Hypocrite! thou shouldst have chosen the fear of God, as thou hast chosen a profession without it; but thou hast cast off fear, because thou art an hypocrite; and because thou art such, thou shalt have the same measure that thou metest. God will cast thee off, because thou art an hypocrite. God hath prepared a fear for thee, because thou didst not choose the fear of God; and that fear shall come upon thee like desolation, and like an armed man, and shall swallow thee up, thou and all that thou art.

Hypocrite! read this text and tremble : "The sinners in Zion are afraid; fearfulness hath surprised the hypocrites. Who among us shall dwell with the devouring fire? who among us shall dwell with everlasting burnings?" Isa. xxxiii. 14.

Hypocrite! thou art not under the fatherly protection of God, because thou art an hypocrite, and wantest his fear in thine heart. The eyes of the Lord are upon those that fear him, to deliver them; but the fearless man is left to the snare and wiles of the devil, to be caught therein and over-come, because he is destitute of the fear of God.

Hypocrite! thou art like to have no other reward of God for thy labour, than that which the goats shall have; the hypocrite shall not stand in God's sight. The gain of thy religion thou spendest as thou gettest it; thou wilt not have one farthing overplus at death and judgment.

Hypocrite! God hath not intrusted thee with the least drachm of his saving grace, nor will he, because thou art an hypocrite. And as for what thou hast, thou hast stolen it, even every man of you from his neigh-bour; still pilfering out of their profession, even as Judas did out of the bag. Thou camest like a thief into thy profession, and like a thief thou shalt go out of the same. Jesus Christ hath not counted thee faithful to commit to thee any of his jewels to keep, because thou fearest him not. He hath given his banner to those that fear him, that it may be dis-played because of the truth.

Hypocrite! thou art not true to God, nor man, nor thine own soul, because thou art an hypocrite. How should the Lord put any trust in thee? Why should the saints look for any good from thee? Should God give thee his word, thou wilt sell it; should men commit their souls to thee, thou wilt de-stroy them, by making merchandize of them for thy own hypocritical designs. Yea, if the sun waxes hot, thou wilt throw all away, and not endure the heat, because thou art an hypocrite.

THE END.

London: Printed by W. Clowes and Sons, Duke Street, Lambeth.

CPSIA information can be obtained
at www.ICGtesting.com
Printed in the USA
BVHW061453050721
610882BV00006B/18